The Quest for the
Green Man

The Quest for the
Green Man

John Matthews

A publication supported by
THE KERN FOUNDATION

Quest Books
Theosophical Publishing House

Wheaton, Illinois ◆ Chennai (Madras), India

QUEST BOOKS
are published by
The Theosophical Society in America,
Wheaton, Illinois 60189–0270,
a branch of a world fellowship,
a membership organization
dedicated to the promotion of the unity of
humanity and the encouragement of the study of
religion, philosophy, and science, to the end that
we may better understand ourselves and our place in
the universe. The Society stands for complete
freedom of individual search and belief.
For further information about its activities,
write, call 1–800–669–1571, e-mail olcott@theosmail.net,
or consult its Web page: http://www.theosophical.org

The Theosophical Publishing House
is aided by the generous support of
THE KERN FOUNDATION,
a trust established by Herbert A. Kern
and dedicated to Theosophical education

For additional information write to
The Theosophical Publishing House
P.O. Box 270
Wheaton, IL 60189–0270
A publication of the Theosophical Publishing House,
a department of the Theosophical Society in America.

Designer: Justina Leitão
Editorial team: Jane Alexander, Katey Day,
Sharron Dorr, Douglas Gillette
Picture researcher: Kay Rowley

To Ari & Kris

for all the reasons they can think of

5/03

Author's acknowledgments

A number of people helped in the research of this book. I
would like especially to thank Dr. Ari Berk for his advice on
Native American traditions and for reading parts of the
manuscript at a crucial time; Nigel Pennick for his expert
help on the Green Man traditions of Germany and Austria;
Janet Piedelato for advice on Egyptian traditions; my wife
Caitlín Matthews for checking the text and commenting
throughout and for designing the wonderful diagram which
appears on page 20; Bill Lewis for permission to quote from
his poem Green Heart on page 130; my editors, Jane
Alexander at Godsfield Press and Douglas Gillette and
Sharron Dorr at Quest; Kay Rowley for her work on the
pictures; Justina Leitão for design; Geraint ap Iorweth for
the picture of the Green Man from Pennel; and last, but by
no means least, long overdue thanks to Eric Barrett, for many
years of generous help in keeping my computer running when
I would have thrown it through the window!

John Matthews, Oxford
Midsummer's Day, 2000

C. 1

Contents

Prelude

The Quest Begins

Green Man dancing
on the may-blossom earth
sings a small song
of the joy of being:
"I am the centre.
I reside not in stone,
but in grass, in leaves—
behind which, smiling,
I keep my council."

John Matthews, *Green Man Turning*

A WONDROUS MYSTERY
The Green Man is a wondrous and mysterious being who wears many disguises—vegetative, animal, human, and suprahuman. For the preliterate world he embodied the unfolding cycle of greenness and growth, the realm of fields, forests, and hedgerows upon which all life depended and without which there could be no food for man or beast. For the civilized world he took other forms: that of a mythological archetype representing the spiritual intelligence of nature; of a character from folklore personifying the eternal round of the agricultural year; of a mythic hero who transcends death to bring us the wisdom of the Otherworld; of a mysterious challenger who demands that we look again at our connection with the world around us. More recently, he has reappeared as a potent symbol of ecological concern.

We may deny the connection between these things, may strip the Green Man to the bare boughs, but what is left still burns in both heart and head. It does so because what the Green Man represents (in the sense of re-presents) is the spirit of nature, of Being itself, overflowing with abundance, both material and spiritual. Strangely, as our ancestors intuited and as we know from our own lives, this abundance is released only through periodic deprivation, challenge, and self-sacrifice. This is the core mystery of the Green Man. Even if we think of him as nothing more than the "energy" of nature, shaped by human imagination, we will not fail to catch the scent of greenness, the lingering trace of something that is no more diminished today than it was when the Green Man first walked into the consciousness of our ancestors in ages past.

ABOVE AND RIGHT: The ancient, all-knowing face of the Green Man looks out at us from amid the leaves in these two images, one a modern carving by Fleur Fitzgerald, the other a medieval roof boss from Norwich Cathedral, England.

ABOVE: *The redwoods represent the power of the Green Man as it comes to us through our interaction with the natural world.*

The story of the Green Man is one of the oldest in the world, though until the rise of civilization it had no written text, appearing instead in the forms of nature and in the many ways that human beings have found to celebrate them. Go out into any part of the land at a high point of the year, but especially in summer between May and June, and you will feel his presence—in the standing corn and the waving wheat, in the rich greenery of the trees, and in the heavy blossoms that decorate the hedgerows. You will even find him in midwinter, when the trees are bare and a chill wind blows through their slumbering boughs.

If you can hear deeply, the earth sings with bounteous energy. When the people of the distant past encountered this energy, they gave it an imaginal form. The shape this virile energy took was, in part, human, and it was green. It represented a harmonious combining of the dynamic energy of human life and the powerful life force of nature, personified in a way that can be recognized and acknowledged by all.

Throughout this book the emphasis is on the Green Man, a masculine archetype. But divinities and spirits who represent the generative powers of the universe appear as complementary energies, masculine and feminine. We should be careful of restricting their influence to contemporary concerns of gender. Gods and archetypes, whether male or female, influence both genders and cannot be restricted to one or the other. Feminine aspects of the energy the Green Man represents abound, consorts both human and divine, who match his power and presence at

many points—the Green Woman, Flower Brides, and the Spring Maidens, without whom the story of the Green Man would be incomplete.

Knowledge and understanding of the Green Man has passed deeply into our human awareness. We see our origins reflected in the creative energy of nature and, with the understanding that human beings possess an unseen dimension that we call "soul," so in turn have we experienced nature as possessing a similar dimension. It may be better to think of the Green Man as a spirit, at once formless but taking many forms. This the Green Man

The story of the Green Man was told and retold in every part of the world in those far-off times, until everyone knew it, not just with mind and memory, but with soul and spirit.

certainly does, endlessly changing and adapting to the circumstances in which he finds himself.

The story of the Green Man was part of our first realizations as a species. It was told and retold in every part of the world in those far-off times, until everyone knew it, not just with mind and memory, but with soul and spirit. That same story is still told today every time the Green Man is remembered, in whatever form he takes; and it is recognized in the continuing rhythms and cycles of nature, which endlessly reiterate his presence and the part he plays in the story of creation.

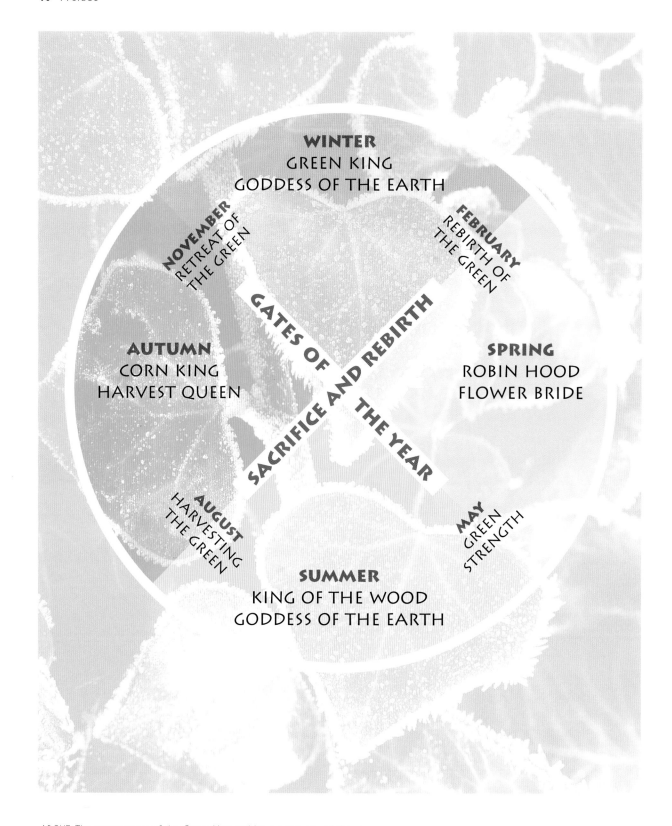

ABOVE: The appearances of the Green Man and his consort around the year.

AN ENDLESS STORY

At his core, the Green Man is indissolubly linked with the vegetative cycle of the year. Here he appears in various guises with his various consorts, shifting shape and identity with the seasons, appearing and disappearing with bewildering skill. This pattern will appear again and again throughout this book, but for the moment we may see it best as a diagram, with the

ABOVE: This second-century head from Am Herrenbrünnchen Roman temple was plundered and placed in Trier Catherdral.

appearances of the Green Man and his consorts set out around the year (left). It is a pattern also found in the oldest stories of the Green Man, where he is represented by dying and rising gods such as Attis, Osiris, Tammuz, and Bran, or in the earliest heroes of whom we know, such as Enkidu from the ancient Sumerian

Epic of Gilgamesh. Later we will see this same shape reflected in the Roman story of the King of the Wood, who ruled for a year, only to be cut down by an opponent who then replaced him as a resurrected reembodiment of the life force he represented.

Not all of the appearances of the Green Man and his consort are represented in this diagram. Indeed, we will have to look far afield to see the pattern in its entirety. We find other stories that hark back to this ancient pattern in the myths of different vegetation gods—Corn Kings and Spring Queens, Lords of the May and Maidens in the Bower. We also see how the archetype manifests in figures such as Green Jack, Robin Hood, Robin Goodfellow, Herne the Hunter, the Green Knight, and characters from the ancient folk plays of Europe.

In each case, though, the story is the same: the god brings the life force to the earth, grows in the grain, is cut down, and springs up again. All these figures are archetypal images of one of the oldest themes of which we have knowledge—death and rebirth. As the old English folk song says of a native Corn King, John Barleycorn:

> There were three men came out of the West
> Their fortunes for to try,
> And these three men made a solemn vow,
> John Barleycorn should die.
>
> They ploughed him in the earth so deep,
> with clods upon his head,
> Then these three men they did conclude
> John Barleycorn was dead.
>
> There he lay sleeping in the ground
> Till rain from the sky did fall;
> Then Barleycorn sprang a green blade
> And proved liars of them all.

The theme is one we can recognize at every level in our own lives. Again and again we see aspects of ourselves—ideas, beliefs, relationships, surroundings—

change and die only to spring up again, reconstituted in the ever shifting drama of our being. In both the inner spiritual reality as well as in the outer circumstances of our lives, the eternal round of birth, growth, death, and rebirth is enacted in myriad different ways.

THE UNDYING SPIRIT

The human spirit itself has proved to be stronger than anyone could ever have imagined. It refuses to die despite the often terrible conditions in which it has existed. The Green Man, too, has proved impossible to kill. Again and again throughout the ages he has returned to remind us of our indissoluble links with nature—often in such a mysterious manner that it is hard to know where to look for him. For he is a trickster too, laughing both with us and at us—with us through the sheer joy of being, and at us in our inability to comprehend and so embody his aliveness in our own lives. Always, he leads us deeper into reality. As a shaman journeying on our behalf into realms to which we might never go, he returns with knowledge vital to our survival.

Often, just when we think we are about to catch him, he shifts his shape and vanishes again, only to reappear in another guise before our wondering eyes. Becoming familiar with some of his disguises and thereby learning to laugh with him and to celebrate his spirit in our spirits is the point of this book.

THE GREEN MAN'S GIFTS

From the Green Man our ancestors learned the secrets of life: the existence of the soul; the idea of the Otherworld and the afterlife; the mystery of the seasons and the agricultural year; the lore of medicinal herbs and plants; the companionship of the natural world. The Green Man's spirit was recognized everywhere in the green and growing world, especially in the dark forests which covered so much of the earth.

The presence of the Green Man expresses an ancient ability to interact with our environment, to take only what we need to survive, and to preserve the rest. It was from this impulse that we learned how to celebrate the mystery of the seasons and how to live in harmony with the fruitful earth.

If we go out into the natural world, if we peer deeply enough and long enough into the myths, legends, and folklore of the many lands where he is known, we can see the Green Man still, dancing a curious springtime dance through the fields, wielding his fearful midwinter ax, staring down at us from strange carvings in the roofs of old churches, or looking out from behind the trees of an ancient wood.

Like all spirits, like Spirit itself, he is as hard to find as a tree in a thicket. He is still, as he always was, an ancient god, a spirit of the woods, a messenger of nature.

The Green Man has been with us for a long time. He has been worshiped, carved, painted, and sculpted out of branches and ferns, praised, reviled, studied, filmed, and sung about. Yet, like all spirits, like Spirit itself, he is as hard to find as a tree in a thicket. He is still, as he always was, an ancient god, a spirit of the woods, a messenger of nature, a guardian and challenger of all who seek him. But behind his many forms is a reality we cannot deny: the presence of the natural world which is everywhere around us and within us, whether we live in a city or a wilderness. For the Green Man is a prophet also, bringing news of what may happen to the world—and to us—if we continue to destroy the natural resources of the earth. Most importantly, he reminds us that we are not the lords of creation, but partners in the vast, living ecosystem that is our planet.

RIGHT: The face of the Green Man looks out from the carvings around this ancient door to Kilpeck Church in Herefordshire.

THE QUEST BEGINS

My own quest for the Green Man has been a long one, stretching back almost twenty years, from the time I first became aware of mysterious leafy faces staring down at me from the roofs and pillars of a country church in Oxfordshire. The search has lead along many strange and wonderful byways—from the ancient theme of fertility and the dying and rising god to the contemporary concerns of ecology. On the way I have spent time in the company of some fascinating figures; but always I feel led back to the strange, staring, mirthful faces hidden among

> . . . and wonderful byways—from the ancient theme of fertility and the dying and rising god to the contemporary concerns of ecology.

the symbols of church and pew which seem to have so much to say about our relationship to the natural world and the environment.

I have found it almost impossible to study the Green Man without thinking of him as a distinct personality. Even the driest academic studies give way to this perspective, so that we constantly encounter poetic rhapsodies on the "humanity" of the Green Man and his foliate heads. I am certainly no exception; and throughout this book I refer to the Green Man as "he," just as I would if I were writing about a historical character, even though I am aware of the limitations of anthropomorphizing archetypes.

In fact, the Green Man is far larger than any simple attempt to define him. He may never have had a single cultural representation, but he has acquired a personality as distinct as that of any living person. I feel I have come to know him as such over the years, and without his tacit agreement, I could never have embarked on this attempt to tell his story.

An old folktale describes the discovery of a human representative of the Green Man in Britain during the Middle Ages. This man was kept in a cage as a kind of freak and never spoke until his death, which came shortly after his incarceration. But the archetypal Green Man has never fallen silent; *we* have merely ceased to hear *him*. It is my belief that we need to pay attention to the things he has to tell us,

ABOVE AND LEFT: A medieval image of the Green Man from Tewkesbury Abbey and a later carving from Crowcombe, Somerset. Each represents a different aspect of his iconography.
RIGHT: A glorious carving of the Green Man from Westminster Abbey, London. His presence was a direct challenge to Christianity.

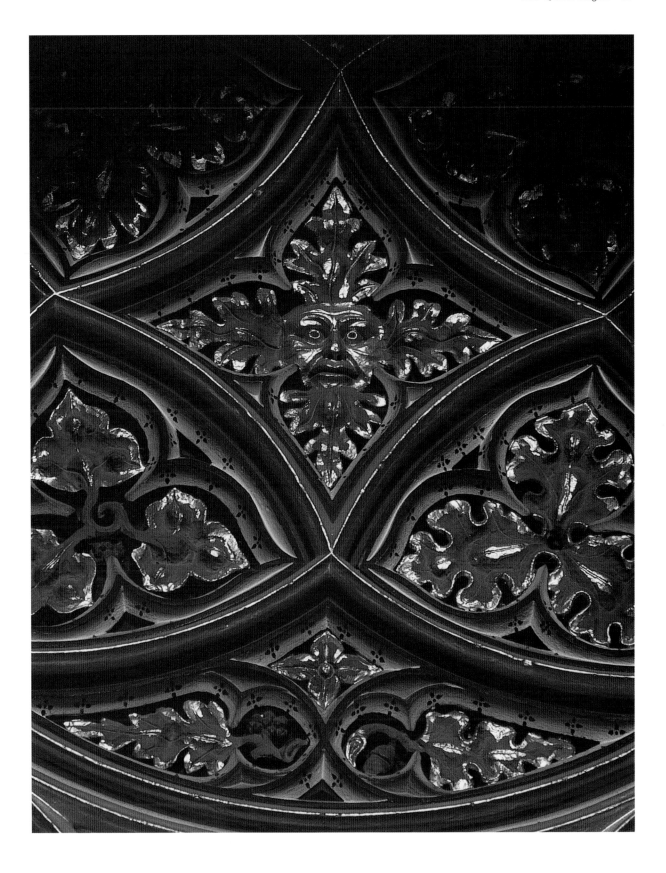

because without that knowledge we ourselves stand in danger of perishing. The purpose of this book is to rediscover the Green Man for our own time, in the foliage of his many forms as well as in the deep recesses of our hearts, to find out—through history, story, art, and personal meditation—what his message is for us today.

He leads us on a merry dance, this leaf-faced being. Maybe he can never be captured, but the pursuit can be both challenging and broadening. What I have learned, from a multitude of sources, is set down here. But it is still "out there" in the wildwoods and green-hung hollows of the land that he hides. Perhaps as you read, you too will become a hunter of the Green Man. If so, be prepared for a wonderful adventure—one that will lead you into many out-of-the-way corners of history and myth. As you go, do not be surprised if you find yourself accompanied, shadowed by the very being you are seeking. For so it seems to have been from the beginning: as we hunt the Green Man, he also hunts us, until we no longer know who is the hunter and who the hunted!

To help you enter his world, you will find a series of brief meditations or other practical suggestions at the end of each chapter. I intend these to help you chart your way though the mysterious realm of the Green Man—to encounter him for yourself. You can follow the meditations as written, or record them if you wish, so that you can experience them more directly. Look for a quiet place, if possible in nature, to try them out. Read or listen and let your spirit follow where the Green Man leads.

ABOVE: A prehistoric shaman in animal disguise represents one of the oldest aspects of the Green Man—guardian of the animals.

THE CHALLENGE OF THE GREEN MAN

The Green Man has been among us for hundreds, even thousands, of years—as far back as the ancient shamans of Europe and North America—certainly as long ago as the astonishing early culture of Mesopotamia where, in the *Epic of Gilgamesh*, we glimpse him in the mighty form of Enkidu, the first representation of the Green Man in epic literature. He is present in the Egyptian myths of Isis and Osiris, in the ancient dances and folk plays of Europe, and in the trickster figures of many other cultures.

The Green Man archetype is unusual in Western culture, where nature is usually thought of as feminine, and men, other than farmers, frequently have a conflicted relationship with the natural world. They have defoliated and cut down the vast rain forests to raise cattle, dropped bombs, contaminated the earth with industrial waste, and otherwise despoiled the world around us. In opposition to this destructive trend, the Green Man has an important role to play in symbolizing the masculine consciousness of Nature.

And he is not as far removed from our everyday lives as it may appear. We find him in contemporary movies about Robin Hood, in the imagery and concerns of the Green Movement, in advertising slogans for Jolly Green Giant vegetables, in modern comic books and fantasy writing, and in private gardens, where contemporary foliate heads are popular ornaments. Even NASA's astronauts, who left the earth as scientists and came home as visionaries proclaiming the message that the earth is alive and sacred, saw the true meaning of the Green Man. The burgeoning Men's Movement has also found a wise and powerful counselor in the person of the Green Man.

ABOVE: This modern tile by John Piper depicts both the secret inner face and the bold outer stare of the Green Man's form.

It seems both ironic and appropriate that with deforestation at a critical high, cultural interest in the Green Man is reemerging. The reason may well be one of those great balancing moves of the collective unconsciousness, or indeed of nature itself, that seem to occur when needed. In terms of the death and rebirth motif characterizing so many myths of the Green Man, it seems fitting that he should reappear now, perhaps as an expression of communal hope that we can remember, revitalize, and redeem our relationship with the natural world.

Chapter One

The Face in the Leaves

Like antlers, like veins of the brain the birches
Mark patterns of mind on the red winter sky;
"I am thought of all plants," says the Green Man,
"I am thought of all plants," says he.

William Anderson, *The Green Man*

Wherever you go among the fields and woodlands, from spring to summer, summer to fall, fall to winter, winter to spring, and so round again, the presence of the Green Man goes with you. His energy is in everything, and his green wisdom surrounds us from dawn to dusk. The life-giving force he represents can guide and direct us, and offers strength to fuel our growth.

THE GREEN GUARDIAN

Among the riot of carvings that decorate so many of the medieval churches and cathedrals of Europe we encounter a strange character: a mocking, half-human face who grins down at us from on high, carved on roof bosses, or who peers out from dark and dusty corners of the building. These carvings, called "foliate heads," are faces that seem human, but that sprout leaves from eyes, lips, nose, and ears. They sometimes seem to be peering from amid the leafage, and at other times to be actually made of leaves. The story behind them dates back to a time before

ABOVE:The sad face of the Green Man from All Saints Church,
Sutton Berenger, England, reflects upon the human condition.
RIGHT: A lone rowan tree represents the green energy of the
earth, ever close to us as we walk upon the land.

recorded history, when our relationship to the natural environment was much closer than it has been at any time since.

The distinguished anthropologist Lady Raglan was the first scholar of the twentieth century to notice the foliate heads. Writing in a 1939 edition of the journal of the English Folklore Society, she described how, eight years previously, the Rev. J. Griffith had shown her a carving on the roof of the church at Llangwm in Monmouthshire. Lady Raglan wrote that the carving was of "a man's face, with oak leaves growing from the mouth and ears, and completely encircling the head. . . . Mr. Griffith suggested that it was intended to symbolize the spirit of inspiration, but it seemed to me certain that it was a man and not a spirit, and moreover that it was a 'Green Man.'"

Convinced that the faces she observed were portraits, Lady Raglan sought a figure from "real life" from which the grinning, leafy faces could derive. But here she was to be disappointed. She concluded: "The answer, I think, is that there is only one [figure] of sufficient importance, the figure variously known as the Green Man, Jack-in-the-Green, Robin Hood, the King of May, and the Garland, who is the central figure in the May Day celebrations throughout Northern and Central Europe."

THE HUNT
ANTLERED STAG
UNICORN
PRIMEVAL FOREST
EARTHLY PARADISE
BROCELIANDE

WINTER
GREEN KNIGHT
BEHEADING GAME
SOLSTICE REVELS
BEASTS OF
MIDWINTER
WASSAILING THE
APPLE TREES

SPIRIT OF THE GREEN
HILDEGARD: VERIDITAS
OF SOUL
ST. FRANCIS: RESPECT
FOR CREATION
GREENING
THE SOUL

WOODCRAFTS
WOOD WISDOM
MUSICAL INSTRUMENTS:
PIPE, HARP, VIOL
SPORTS: CRICKET, HURLEY
WOOD TRAVEL: SHIPS,
CORACLES, CARTS

REFRESHMENT OF NATURE
TREE SHADE
SANCTUARY OF THE GROVE
UNTRAMMELED BY CARE
HOLIDAY
HOLY DAY
OPEN SPACE
FRESH AIR

GAMES
DANCE OF THE SEASONS
FAIR PLAY AND CHALLENGE
GWYDDBWYLL
FIDCHELL
CHESS

AUTUMN
JOHN BARLEYCORN
THE BATTLE OF THE FIELDS
CORN DOLLIES

DEITIES
ADONIS
ATTIS
TAMMUZ
OSIRIS
CHRIST
ODIN
INANNA
ISHTAR
APHRODITE

GREEN IN BODY
GROWTH
SAP
PHOTOSYNTHESIS
DANCE
SEXUALITY
ENGAGEMENT WITH LIFE

SPRING
WEARING THE GREEN
JACK-IN-THE-GREEN
MAY DAY REVELS
MAID MARIAN
ROBIN HOOD

CHAMPION OF THE GODDESS
CUCHULLIN
GAWAIN
GILGAMESH
MORRIGHAN
MORGAN LE FAY
ISHTAR

FOLIATE HEADS
WODEWOSE
HERNE
WILD HERDSMEN
REX NEMORENSIS
THRESHOLD
GUARDIAN
GENIUS OF
THE FOREST

SUMMER
MORRIS
DANCERS
BERRYMEN
GARLAND DAY
CHARLES II IN
OAK TREE

WILDNESS
SUIBHNE GELT
MERLIN
ENKIDU
SWEET LADY
GUINEVERE
LADY OF THE
FOUNTAIN

ABOVE: Some of the many faces and names of the Green Man through the ages.

Lady Raglan had, in fact, discovered the truth: the Green Man exists not just in historical time, or in medieval sculpture, but as a living presence whom many still acknowledge today.

EARLY GLIMPSES OF THE GREEN MAN

From these brief and inconclusive remarks has sprung a veritable forest of notions concerning the identity of the mysterious leafy faces. They have been studied at length by an increasing number of researchers, each of whom records his or her first encounter with the Green Man in terms of wonder which soon turns to passionate curiosity. They have found within the lore surrounding this figure a huge spectrum of personal meaning, ranging from feelings of nostalgia for a past long dead to the inspired recognition of the Green Man as the spirit of nature.

The late Kathleen Basford, who made the first detailed study of the foliate heads, describes her intriguing encounter with one in the ruins of Fountains Abbey in Yorkshire this way:

One day, wandering round the ruins, I happened to glance up at one of the tall windows of the Chapel of the Nine altars and noticed, near the apex of the arch, the carving of a human head with a weird growth of vegetation coming out of the mouth. . . . The sad face of this withered old man seemed to me the most human touch left in the ruins and yet, at the same time, the most ghostly.

Though her expertise was in botany and genetics, Mrs. Basford became haunted by the carving and was filled with a desire to discover more. Equipped with the necessary photographic equipment, she set forth on a twelve-year quest that resulted in one of the best collections of photographs on the subject so far and with the publication of her book in 1978. She

ABOVE: *One of the oldest surviving images of the Green Man: a carving from a temple-palace in Hatra, Iraq.*
ABOVE LEFT: *The foliate head from Fountains Abbey, Yorkshire.*

concluded that the medieval carvings originated in classical art, the earliest examples of which date from the end of the first century AD. No more than male masks with acanthus leaves sprouting from their faces, these early carvings are little more than sketches for what was to come.

Dating from the early Roman period, we find faces that either sprout or are decorated with leaves all over the western and eastern parts of what once was the Roman Empire, in places as far apart as Baalbek in the Lebanon and Bordeaux in France. Further east, a prototype of the Green Man appears on the facade of a temple at Hatra, the ancient heart of the great Mesopotamian empire now in modern Iraq. The reason for its appearance here is no accident, as we shall see. Though none of these images expresses the fullness of the archetype as portrayed in Europe, they offer important additional clues to the Green Man's character.

THE SPIRIT OF THE TREES

These early manifestations of the Green Man certainly did not originate in the classical or medieval worlds. His true origins lie in the spiritual intuitions of tribal peoples living in the vast woods that once covered most of the European continent. He is, in part, a spirit of these woods, a representation, in semi-human form, of the abiding life force of the trees.

We often forget just how extensive the forests of Europe were. Much of the Continent and extensive areas of Britain and Ireland were covered in a dense, almost impenetrable cloak of trees. For the ancient peoples who inhabited these areas, woodland and forest spirits were everywhere. It is small wonder that these peoples acknowledged them as deities of power and importance. Trees had been honored from very ancient times, and this honoring was carried over into the Celtic period. During this period we find lists of trees with particular spiritual attributes, attributes that represent a complex interweaving of symbols. This Celtic tree symbolism adds a further dimension

BELOW: The face of the Green Man appears in the folds and creases of bark from a great tree.
BELOW RIGHT: The eyebrows and hair sprout like leaves on this early Celtic head from Heidelberg, Germany.

RIGHT: Yggdrasil, the Norse world tree, is the foundation of creation itself. Like many trees in the ancient world, it was honored almost as a god.

to the mythology of the Green Man.

It is scarcely surprising that trees should be regarded as sacred. Not only are they the largest manifestation of the vegetative world, but they can also be seen as connecting the three levels of existence universally acknowledged by traditional peoples. The tree's roots go down into the body of the earth, the mother of all and the repository of the ancient dead. The branches of the tree stretch high up into the heavens, the home of the gods. The trunk of the tree creates a bridge between these two otherworldly dimensions and the material world we inhabit.

Trees must also have seemed virtually immortal, in some cases living for as long as two thousand

At tree shrines, rites were celebrated that honored

the trees themselves and the gods they represented.

years. Their human-like appearance—the "body" of the trunk, the "arms" of the branches, and the twig-like "fingers," all held within the skin of the bark and animated by blood-like sap—added to their personification as including yet transcending the human realm. They must have powerfully invoked the presence of the Green Man himself.

We find sacred trees in many cultures. Yggdrasil in the Norse Tradition is the world tree on which the world is founded; Eo Mugna in Irish tradition is considered a source of Druidic and territorial power; in the Mediterranean cult of Cybele and Attis, the pine signified the death and rebirth of the god.

Trees were also considered to possess the qualities of the deities to which they were dedicated, and we hear much of tree shrines where rites were celebrated that honored not only the trees themselves but also the gods they represented.

The sacred oak groves of the Druids are well known. They were the subject of debate and struggle as the advancing tide of Christianity strove to outlaw the older "pagan" ways. Many ancient oak groves were cut down by the Christians as a sign that the ancient traditions no longer held sway. However, the felling of the groves often reinforced their power in the imaginations of those who resisted the Church's advance. For these people, trees became a sign of rebellion against the new religion.

A story is told about the great churchman St. Patrick, who commanded his followers to cut down some trees to build a new church. They chose to fell the trees of an ancient sacred grove, and when

Patrick heard this, he insisted the trees be left where they had fallen and new ones cut down from the forest. He later said that the worst sound he could ever hear was that of an ax hitting a sacred tree in Ireland. This is a tribute to the respect he felt for the pre-Christian Irish culture, even though he had come to drive out the pagan religion.

Pre-Christian beliefs did not simply cease because the Church told people the woods were full of evil. In fact, it was in acknowledgment of the importance of the forest that so many medieval churches were designed to look like stone forests. Nor should we forget that the scaffolding to support the masonry was made of wood. Actually, it is hardly surprising that a place was found for the Green Man in church architecture. The fact is that he was too deeply embedded in the consciousness of the ordinary people to be forgotten. Of course, the churchmen could dismiss him as a reminder of demonic forces—the so-called "damned in the demon-wood"—but the foliate heads remained as a constant reminder of older forces at work in the world.

CELTIC HEADS

Seeking inspiration from a classical heritage, the medieval masons probably began by copying the early Roman leaf masks; but they added details of their own. They were almost certainly influenced in this emergent iconography by representations of the human head dating from

RIGHT: One of the oldest carvings of the Green Man: a Celtic pillar from Pfalzfeld, Germany.

the Roman occupation of Britain, when classical depictions of deity became intermingled with the beliefs of the native population—the Celts. Many of these carvings are still to be seen on ancient crosses and gravestones from medieval times.

The importance of the human head to the Celtic peoples is well known. They regarded it as the seat of the soul, and they took the heads of defeated enemies to display as trophies—a distant notion that may well be echoed in the foliate heads suspended in the roof-trees of Christian churches.

The Celts made few images of deity before they encountered classical Greece and Rome, but when they did so, the images they most often chose were heads. Indeed, what may be one of the oldest extant Green Man heads is found on a carved stone pillar from Pfalzfeld, Germany. Although this is not a true foliate head, the eyebrows seem to sprout, and the whole pillar is ornately decorated with greenery.

These early carved heads were certainly of religious significance, and in some instances they represent specific gods. The most easily identifiable is a horned figure often identified as Cernunnos, a god whose history is fragmentary, but who is represented as having a special connection with animals and the natural world.

We catch a glimpse of him on a wonderful relief on the Gunderstrup Cauldron, a Celtic artifact discovered in a Danish bog in the 1930s. This image is identified as Cernunnos in the guise of an antlered shaman surrounded by spirit animals. The shamanic connection is one we will revisit; it ties in well

with two more strands in the Green Man's character—his possession of horns and his distillation of native wisdom. Horned figures are very much a part of the Green Man's ever changing form, and like the shamans who drew upon the energy he represented, he was often sought out in times of trial for whatever knowledge he was willing to share.

Celtic heads proliferate throughout Britain and France, but one of the most striking is the great head displayed on the pediment of the Roman temple in Bath. This carving almost certainly depicts the head of Bran the Blessed, a Celtic demigod, in his guise as the sun and as a keeper of wisdom.

Bran, whose story we encounter in the great storehouse of native British myth known as the *Mabinogion*, is both a warrior and a god. In the story of "Branwen Daughter of Llyr," we learn that, having

ABOVE: The head of Bran the Blessed from the Romano-British temple at Bath, England. His severed head became oracular.

received a poisoned wound in battle, Bran orders his followers to cut off his head and preserve it on a secret island. There it continues to speak, relaying stories and traditions to all who stand before it.

Indeed, Bran is one of several such beings referenced in Celtic tradition whose heads, when severed, become oracular. These ancient figures were seen as storehouses of wisdom, as keepers of the teachings and traditions of earlier times. Their continued vitality after beheading shows them to have been a symbolic representation of the dying and rising god we will encounter again and again throughout this book. These heads are not usually decorated with leaves and so are not—in Raglan and Basford's technical sense—foliate heads; nevertheless, they embody a source of instinctual wisdom that, in the later carvings, presents itself as a torrent of abundant leafage. This exhalation of leaves conveys the truth that the Green Man communicates to us not in words but in the imagery of vegetation.

The fact that many of the medieval foliate heads are tricephalic (three headed) may owe itself to the Celtic love of triplicates reflected in more than one of the carvings. If a single one was powerful, three were more powerful still, and collections of references—called "triads"—to mystical and magical events abound in the written literature of the Celts.

Another figure in Celtic imagery may be discerned in a Romano-Celtic inscription to a god named Veridius, (a word meaning "Green") found at Ancaster in Lincolnshire. This inscription, despite being written in Latin, probably refers to an older Celtic deity absorbed into Roman tradition. His importance to the people of this area was sufficient to garner him a temple, the pediment of which the inscription once adorned.

The symbolic importance among the Celts of the color green itself is further suggested by the body of a warrior, one of the so-called bog bodies found preserved in the Lindow moss in Cheshire. Traces of pigment found on the body suggest that it may have been painted green after death—symbolizing the return of the flesh to the earth as well as the presence of a "green energy" within the human shell.

Perhaps here we catch a glimpse of a more intimate connection between the Green Man and his human counterparts. Both were linked closely with the energy of the earth in all its forms, most especially as these manifested through the imagery of growth and renewal.

GREENING THE GREEN MAN

But the Celts were by no means the first people to discover the Green Man. The further back in time we go, the more aware we become of a whole array of his ancient, archetypal relatives. These trace an unwavering thread of continuity back through the great civilizations of the world, repeating over and over the central themes of the story: the birth, rise, death, and rebirth of the god, paralleled by our own ever-more-tenuous connection with the natural world. Each figure adds to the emerging picture of the manifest intelligence of nature, which we begin to see ever more clearly as we follow the ancient archetype through its many and varied appearances.

The presence of the foliate heads discovered at Hatra leads us to the figure of Enkidu in the *Epic of Gilgamesh* (c 700 BC). Enkidu is a wild and primitive being who possesses great strength and a passionate

ABOVE: A contemporary cast of the Green Man by Allen Calvin shows his most trickster-like face.

and seemingly ungovernable soul. Representing untamed, overflowing life, Enkidu stands forth as one of the oldest images of the potent energy that is inherent to the Green Man and such an essential aspect of our own lives.

In the story, Enkidu and his friend, the great hero-king Gilgamesh, undertake many adventures together, including the slaying of the Bull of Heaven.

This angers the gods, and Enkidu is condemned to die. Enkidu's death, and an awareness of his own mortality, prompt Gilgamesh to undertake a journey to the Otherworld in search of a cure for death itself, a plant called "The Old Man has Become a Young Man Again." Although Gilgamesh finds the plant, he loses it again to a serpent, which at once sloughs its skin in a potent symbolic image of rebirth. Thus, in this

climactic scene, Enkidu's irrepressible wildness—his "greenness"—while not fully recoverable by human beings, is nevertheless affirmed for nature as a whole.

Later we find this same unvanquishable greenness expressed in the religion of ancient Egypt, which was itself heavily influenced by Sumerian and Mesopotamian beliefs. For the Egyptians, the color green was so positively associated that "to do green things" came to mean doing good, while "to do red things" meant to do evil. Osiris, perhaps the most important deity in Egyptian life, was a god of vegetation and resurrection. His epithet in the Pyramid Texts was "The Great Green," and he frequently appears green skinned as a symbol of resurrection and life. His death and return to life were intimately connected with the flooding of the Nile delta, by which the

ABOVE: Green Isis nurses her son Horus, who was himself protected by a sacred green snake known as Wadjet.

In a potent cycle of dismemberment, death, and resurrection, green Osiris is said to "become" Horus, the child of his marriage to Isis. Horus himself is protected by Wadjet, the green snake, known as "the papyrus colored one." Elsewhere, Isis, his mother, also has a green aspect.

So in Egypt the color green was associated with the feminine as well as the masculine, giving us what are perhaps the earliest recorded appearances of the consort of the Green Man—the Green Woman. This of course relates back to the very first stirrings of awareness in our ancient ancestors, who, as we have seen, perceived the energy of life as a subtle interaction between masculine and feminine, god and goddess, Green Man and Green Woman.

Therefore in ancient Egyptian mythology the goddess Nut is occasion-

fields were greened with new growth. To symbolize the perennial resurrection of the green world, mummy cases representing Osiris were sown with grain and left in the rain so the grain would sprout—a graphic demonstration of life rising from death.

LEFT: The ancient Egyptian god Osiris represents the eternally renewing face of nature. He is often depicted with a green skin.

ally depicted as green because of her part in the creation of all life. Indeed, it could be said that both she and Nun, the creation goddess, who in turn gave birth to Nut, signified the Green Lady whose life force flowed through the world. We could see Nun, the watery abyss, and her child Nut, who personified the starry heavens, as forming a circle in which the green life force quickens everything.

ABOVE: This painting from an Egyptian tomb shows the tree goddess Hathor feeding the dead from a sacred sycamore tree.

The Egyptians also worshiped a powerful tree goddess, Hathor, who appears on a tomb painting from the fourteenth century BC. There she is seen feeding the dead from her home in a sycamore, thus connecting the idea of the Green Woman energy with that of sacred trees, which is such an important part of the Green Man's own iconography.

In each case the importance of the color green cannot be overemphasized. Green is experienced as the color of life itself because it signifies growth and the verdant energy of nature. It is the color of rebirth and resurrection.

In Arabic culture, too, which originated in the area of the world once part of the vast Mesopotamian empires, we often find references to al-Khidr, or "the Green Thing," a figure who began life as the center of a vegetation cult that flowered again much later. In the Koran (18:59–81), Khidir is the mysterious spiritual guide—known as the "Companion"—to both Alexander the Great and Moses. As such, he functions almost as a kind of shaman, offering a direct connection to God. His name may be translated as the Verdant—or "Green"—One. He is perceived as a representative of nature and as a source of supernatural wisdom who lives both inside and outside time and is therefore immortal.

One source describes his having dived into the Well of Life in order to live forever—an image that could easily come from a dozen descriptions of shamanic activity. In each instance the shaman enters the Underworld, a place of ancestral wisdom, and returns with the information he has gathered. This aspect of the Green Man is an important part of the puzzle: his roots go deep into the earth and he is possessed of all the wisdom stored there.

The green color associated with Khidir is also the spiritual color of Islam. Paradise itself is said to be green, and the twelfth, or "hidden" *imam*, a spiritual leader who will appear sometime in the future, is described as living on a green island in a sea of whiteness. Green thus represents divine wisdom in Islamic culture, and those who bear its color or who are symbolically associated with it are especially holy.

ABOVE: Khidir and Elijah at the Fountain of Life. One of the great visionary figures of Islam, Khidir is associated with the color green.

We can see, then, that Khidir represents the Green Man in his spiritual aspect.

Each of these figures, as well as those discussed below, represent the same qualities later discerned in the European Green Man. The evidence as a whole points not only to the symbolic importance of the color green but also to the need for archetypes that represent that greenness. For example, in that part of the world where water was scarce and the miracle of the Nile delta was essential to the sustaining of life, it is scarcely surprising to find green gods and goddesses playing such an important part in spirituality.

GREEN DIONYSUS

In the culture of classical Greece the prime representative of the Green Man is Dionysus (the Roman Bacchus), a deity of nature and agriculture before his later association with wine and ecstasy. In the blending of these two strands of his being he comes very close to the heart of the Green Man.

The orgiastic celebrations in his honor, in which virtually every law governing human nature was abandoned in the search for ecstatic union with the god, made him at once the most feared and beloved of the divinities. Indeed, he represented an abandonment to the power of nature that was later to reemerge in the West in the medieval figure of the Wildman (see chapter 6).

Like Osiris among the Egyptians, Dionysus fostered agriculture among the Greeks, and his power manifests often in images of growth and wildness. At one point in his career he is said to have undertaken a journey to India, spreading the word about the intoxication of the fruit of the vine as he went. On the journey he was captured by some sailors, who tried to ransom him for a vast sum. In response Dionysus caused a huge grape vine to grow out of the deck of their ship, and ivy and vines to twine through the rigging. The oars became serpents and the whole ship filled with animals—with the god, in lion form, as their lord. As we will see later, this lord-of-the-animals theme is another aspect of the nature of the Green Man.

In yet another account, Dionysus becomes an old man and passes into the Underworld in search of knowledge. While he undertakes this shamanic activity he is known as Okeanus, in which form he appears as a bearded head, wreathed in ivy and vines.

Like the Green Man, Dionysus is also a dying and rising god. In some versions of his story he is torn apart by jealous gods, only to grow again from his heart, which had been saved by Athena.

RIGHT: Dionysus, the ancient Greek version of the Green Man, dances ecstatically with flute-playing maenads.

ABOVE: *The Eastern face of the Green Man carved into a living banyan tree shows his importance in many cultures.*

GREEN MEN IN ASIA

Perhaps Dionysus's journey to India, which is clearly an account of the passing of religious traditions from one land to another, planted seeds of its own in that far-off land. For, although the Green Man is less ubiquitous in the East than he is in Europe, his presence can be detected in the Indian subcontinent still, as it can in Indonesia and Borneo.

Throughout the region of Apo Kayam in Borneo, a consistent symbol of good luck and fertility is a face sprouting roots and flowers. Found above doors and woven into the baskets in which the native women carry their babies, it may well be a variation of Kirtimukha, an ancient deity of vegetation carved into the temples of the Jain religion throughout

India. Indeed, the entire Jain temple at Ranakpur is designed as a forest in stone somewhat like the cathedrals of Europe, and several Green Man-like faces can be seen amid the leaves.

When the Muslims converted the Jain temple at Qutb Minar into a mosque during the Mogul empire, they left the face of the Green Man carved on its outer walls untouched, although they removed all of the other images. This confirms the idea that the Green Man, in whatever form, was known and respected in the Arab world.

Throughout the East, the colors blue and green are virtually interchangeable, both representing life. Deities of blue or green skin abound. In India we find the blue-skinned Krishna, eighth avatar of Vishnu, the preserving deity of life who is sometimes called "the Supreme Pervader." Krishna is the destroyer of all pain who brings ecstatic communion with the heavenly beings. With his flute he brings delight to the earth, in the manner of Orpheus or the Southwest American Kokopelli, and is shown surrounded by female devotees. He is associated with the first months of spring.

An earlier avatar of Vishnu, the great Rama, whose skin is dark or green, incarnates specifically to overcome the demon Ravana. Rama lives in the woods and takes Sita as his wife, she who springs up from the ground when the earth is ploughed. Such is Rama's beauty, the Hindu scriptures say, that birds, beasts, animals, insects, trees, flowers, and creepers grow sick with longing to draw near and touch him.

GREEN MEN WATCHING

In her brief article Lady Raglan refers to Sir George Fraser's definitive book, *The Golden Bough* (1936), the first really comprehensive study of world mythology and spirituality. What most interested Lady Raglan about Fraser's work were his theories about the Year King, whose human representative was chosen to reign for a year, then killed (usually by decapitation) and hung on a tree. So much symbolism and tradition lies beneath this image that it is not easy to find a path through the undergrowth. But as we shall see, this theme is central in the story of the Green Man, who has had to die before he could be reborn at key points in our history as a visible reminder of our relationship with the natural world.

We cannot say for certain how many of these ancient themes and images were in the minds of the masons who carved the first foliate heads. They may have been stirred by memories, however hazy and

With his flute he brings delight to the earth, in the manner of Orpheus or the Southwest American Kokopelli.

ABOVE: Dionysus in his wildman aspect is a guardian of animals.
LEFT: A Roman mosaic from Cirencester, England, shows Acteon summoning animals to join in his eternal dance of life.

indistinct, of these and other ancient forms. Nor is it hard to believe that these craftsmen saw in the pagan imagery of the Green Man a chance to express the Christian story of death and resurrection in terms that would be familiar to ordinary people for whom doctrine and theology were then far from accessible.

For the medieval churchmen, the symbolism was something other. In the man-made forests of the gothic cathedrals the Green man is pent, the old pagan wildness tamed in stone. If the foliate heads indeed derive from older, pagan

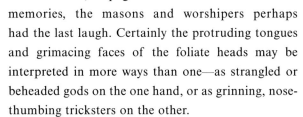

memories, the masons and worshipers perhaps had the last laugh. Certainly the protruding tongues and grimacing faces of the foliate heads may be interpreted in more ways than one—as strangled or beheaded gods on the one hand, or as grinning, nose-thumbing tricksters on the other.

GREEN MEN HIDING

Interestingly, the Green Man emerged more fully as his original home shrank. The steady deforestation of the land, which began with early humankind and continued throughout the medieval period, gained ever greater strength with the growth in population, which required more and more timber for housing.

During the Middle Ages, as if in response to this erosion of his territory, the Green Man metamorphosed into the figure of Robin Hood, who may or may not have been an actual person, but who now became a new representative of the archetype—opposing the ruthlessly enforced forestry laws of the Norman ruling class and behaving in a manner that identifies him as a trickster, one of many traditional figures who have much to do with the creation of life

and with the subsequent response of the gods to the behavior of their creations.

Another figure from the greenwood mythos, a cross between Shakespeare's Puck and a primitive aspect of Green Man, is commonly known as Robin Goodfellow, one of many alternately helpful and malicious spirits who can be found in mythology all over the world. The use of trickery by these spirits is a means of encouraging the psychological and spiritual development of human beings. We will encounter this idea again later when we come to look at some of the various tricky beings who manifest the influence of the Green Man.

THE TEMPLAR CONNECTION

Another place where the presence of the Green Man becomes apparent at this time is in the stories relating to the group of medieval warrior monks known as the Templars. This organization, which began in 1099, initially served as a guardian of the pilgrims making the dangerous journey to Jerusalem. As the crusades got under way, the nature of the Templars changed, until they became a much feared military arm of the Church.

During the next 150 years the Templars accrued great wealth and power, until finally King Philip IV of France, accusing them of heresy, led a concerted attack upon them. The Templars were brutally and efficiently stamped out in 1307, leaving behind many

ABOVE: The almost hidden face of the Green Man looks down from a tree at a circle of ecstatic dancers.
RIGHT: The modern spirit of the Green Man, as portrayed by artist Brian Froud.

strange and intriguing stories about the nature of their spiritual beliefs and practices.

One of the many heretical acts of which they were accused was the worship of a disembodied head, called Baphomet. Recent research has suggested it may have been the mummified head of John the Baptist. Whatever the truth, Baphomet almost certainly evoked for many people the image of the Green Knight, whom we will meet shortly, or even of the carved oracular heads of Celtic times.

The ultimate purpose of the Templar head remains obscure, but at least one use was said to be "to make the earth flower and trees bear fruit." A major Templar foundation, the famed Rosslyn Chapel near Edinburgh, has a very large number of Green Man carvings, which may further suggest that the Templars recognized the Green Man as an ancient

ABOVE: The templar church at Rosslyn, Scotland, has more than one hundred Green Man carvings, a reflection of the importance of the symbol for this elite body of warrior monks.
RIGHT: Felicity Bower's contemporary image of the Green Man.

source of their idiosyncratic beliefs. Certainly their contact with the beliefs of their Arab opponents may also have provided fertile soil in which the notion of a verdant head may have taken root.

RETURN OF THE GREEN MAN

Toward the end of the Middle Ages and into the seventeenth and eighteenth centuries, the story of the Green Man took several new turns. He resurfaced in the more aggressive figure of the Wildman, whose presence personified a reaction to the rapidly diverging worlds of nature and civilization. As humankind became further and further disconnected from its natural environment, more deeply submerged in the Age of Reason, so the natural world became personified as darker and more dangerous.

At the same time, outgrowing the older figure of Robin Hood of Sherwood, the Green Man began to be identified with crude, jester-like figures, called "Greenmen"; these men appeared in numerous English pageants. In addition, he became synonymous with the "Green Jack," a leading character in the folk plays and dances which were still celebrated throughout Britain. To this day, his human representatives may be seen among the "mummers" or folk dancers who come out at key times of the year to portray the ancient myths of the dying and rising god, of the loss and restoration of the green energy of life itself. In addition, images of the Green Man still decorate inn signs all over the country.

Most recently, the Green Man has returned through a resurgence of interest in "green living" and in the works of contemporary fantasists. The immensely popular *Mythago* sequence by Robert Holdstock, the wonderful urban fantasies by Canadian writer Charles de Lint, and even the character of Treebeard in J. R. R. Tolkien's *Lord of the Rings*, have brought the presence of the Green Man back into our midst. Additionally, we have seen his return in a variety of new guises—from comic book heroes such as Green Lantern, Green Arrow, and Slaine, to the presence of the horned spirit known as Herne the Hunter in the popular TV series "Robin of Sherwood." All of these help keep us aware of the character and purpose of the Green Man.

Nor is this the end of the story, for the Green Man refuses to lie down. His story has become inseparable from the wholesale devastation of the environment in our own time, making him an unofficial icon for the modern ecological movement. If anything could be said to represent the spirit of nature and wildness that has been so steadily and completely encroached upon, it is the leafy, laughing, angrily mocking presence of the Green Man. His return to our awareness is much needed. It is my hope that this book may help to restore the Green Man to his original place in our consciousness as the hugely important and eternal figure he is and to see him honored once again.

The following chapters will examine various traditions that show the many aspects of the Green Man in which his message has been preserved, along with the parallel theme of our own currently endangered connection to the natural world.

The Wildman's presence personified a reaction to the rapidly diverging worlds of nature and civilization.

MAKING A SHRINE TO THE GREEN MAN

Many ways exist to celebrate the presence of the Green Man in our lives. The most important remains going out into nature and making a real effort to relate to it—by tuning in to a tree, river, hill, forest, or whatever aspect of the land most draws us. By being in the outside world, we are close to the Green Man; and if we only attune just a little bit at a time, we will begin to feel his energy stirring within us, too.

We might also wish to invite the Green Man into our homes, where his presence and energy can bring us strength and wisdom on a regular basis. The best way to do so is by creating a small inside shrine (which you could also do in your garden).

Just how elaborate you make your shrine is up to you. At a simple level, it could be nothing more than a picture of any aspect of the Green Man that speaks to you, with a votive candle placed before it. Spending a little time each day considering your life in the light of the Green Man's presence may lead to transformative insights. For a more elaborate shrine, you could use natural elements such as stones, earth, and plants to create a permanent reminder of the green energy that is in everything.

You could make this a setting for other Green Man images as well. Many craftspeople make masks or foliate heads or more elaborate sculptures of, for example, Green Men and Green Women, Herne the Hunter, and Cernunnos; many artists have painted wonderful portraits. Inspired by such resources, you could make a lasting and powerful centerpiece in your home, inviting the Green Man to be present. The next few chapters of this book end with suggestions for meditations that you could practice as you sit or stand before your shrine. Or, you could create an affirmation of your own devising, acknowledging the Lord of the Green.

More simply still, you might plant a small spring garden for the Green Man in the depths of winter by covering a small bowl with moss and planting it with spring bulbs. When the shoots show, you are helping to celebrate the bursting forth of energy that the Green Man represents. The custom of planting such miniature sacred gardens is reminiscent of the sprouting tombs of Osiris mentioned above. It was also practiced by the Greeks and Syrians. The tradition continues today in the Christian community, in which children plant Easter gardens in small bowls. As the bulbs show their shoots, so the resurrection of Christ is celebrated.

> Spending a little time each day considering your life in the light of the Green Man's presence may lead to transformative insights.

However you choose to honor the Green Man, remember that he is first and foremost a spirit of nature; while you may wish to make room for him in your home, his true place is in the natural world. You may learn more from a walk in the country than from a hundred meditations. Nor should you forget that wild places exist in our cities, too. Encouraging the planting of trees and their care and protection, creating gardens and parks in your neighborhood, making and maintaining window boxes outside your apartment—all such activities bring something of the Green Man's energy into the stony wilderness where we need it most.

RIGHT: An imaginative reconstruction of a Celtic shrine at a natural spring shows a horned Cernunnos-type figure.

Chapter Two

The King of the Wood

Rise as the sun: antlered—
bearded with greenery—the leaf-vein pulsing
in your throat. Budded all over with small flame,
and motley with birds in your hair and arms.
Rise, and put on your foliage!

Ronald Johnson, *The Book of the Green Man*

The people of the ancient world believed that in order to encourage the earth to bear fruit every season, sacrifices must be made. At one time, living beings were killed to ensure the fecundity of the land. In later times this practice was replaced by a symbolic enactment of the struggle between two aspects of the Green Man—the champions of Summer and Winter—for the goddess of Spring. Today, we also should honor the energy of the turning year and acknowledge all it brings, for the ancient dream of the seasons holds messages we too can read—messages about how to feel, and be, alive; about the self-sacrifices we are required to make in order to do so; about the meaning of our earthly lives; and about how to transcend our physical deaths and live forever in the spirit.

THE GOLDEN KING

The worldwide myth of the sacrificed god-king contains one of the oldest and most important representatives of the Green Man, known to the Romans as the *Rex Nemorensis*, or the "King of the Wood." The human embodiment of this figure was a priest who was elected to reign for a year, at the end of which time he was killed—his slayer taking on the archetypal role of the King for a further year.

This annual "death" and "rebirth" of the King portrayed the eternal round of the seasons, just as the growing corn's harvest and replanting served as a statement of the contract between humanity and the gods who, if propitiated rightly, sent down the rays of the sun to bless the earth and bring forth a new crop ever year. The blood of the slain priest/king was a reminder of humankind's essential relationship to creation and of its debt to the gods.

Sir James George Fraser first drew attention to the figure of the King of the Wood in the *The Golden Bough*. He presents a huge amount of evidence for the King, who fights to be a worthy consort of the goddess Diana. As we will see, this pattern also appears in Celtic story and British folk-ritual

ABOVE: A powerful Green Man from Bamberg Cathedral, Germany. This acanthus-leaf mask acts as a corbel to a foliated ledge.
RIGHT: Spring woodland shows the face of nature at its kindest.

survivals, where a pair of human combatants fight to win a human representative of the May Queen or Flower Bride, who is herself a reflection of the great Goddess. Fraser's classic description of the sacred rite that took place in the Alban hills near Rome at the Temple of Diana is both dramatic and powerful. He writes:

In the sacred grove there grew a certain tree round which at any time of day, and probably far into the night, a grim figure might be seen to prowl. In his hand he carried a drawn sword, and he kept peering wildly about him as if at every instance he expected to be set upon by an enemy. He was a priest and a murderer; and the man for whom he looked was sooner or later to murder him and hold the priesthood in his stead. Such was the rule of the sanctuary. A candidate for the priesthood could only succeed to office by slaying the priest, and having slain him, he retained his office until he was himself slain by a stronger and craftier priest . . . and if he slew him he reigned in his stead with the title of King of the Wood.

In his portrayal of the King of the Wood, Fraser drew on traditions from all over the world, including the Celtic peoples of Britain, Ireland, and Gaul. In particular, he indicated the large number of celebrations that centered on two periods of the year: spring and autumn. These two gateways were seen as key turning points in the progression of the seasons, and it is during this time that the most significant sacrificial acts were observed.

A central instance of these sacrifices was the burning of huge human-shaped wickerwork cages containing human and animal sacrifices. These sacred rites, according to an account by Julius Caesar, took place at May Day and Midsummer, dates that retained their importance even after the Celts became, at least nominally, Christianized. After the abolishment of human sacrifice, these rituals were replaced by ceremonies in which human actors portrayed the King and Queen of the Wood and no actual bloodshed occurred.

GARLANDS FOR THE KING

The timing of these rites is no accident. As we saw earlier, May Day and Midsummer are key points in

Wildness lying just beneath the skin of the land surfaces in feasting and merrymaking and in the dramatic reenactment of an ancient sacrifice.

RIGHT: The Druids offered sacrifices to the gods in wicker cages which were set on fire. Here modern Druids reenact this ceremony.

the progression of the Green Man around the year (see page 10) as they are also key points in the agricultural year. Many of the celebrations in which the Green Man and his representatives are major players still take place around this time.

A ceremony that clearly reflects the older sacrificial rites found a home in the little village of Castleton, which nestles at the head of the Hope Valley in Derbyshire, England. Here, since 1749, "Garland Day" has been celebrated on the 29th of May. Then, the wildness lying just beneath the skin of the land surfaces in feasting and merrymaking and in the dramatic reenactment of an ancient sacrifice.

An eyewitness account from 1901 gives a vivid description of the events of the day and offers a number of valuable clues to the role of the Green Man, then and now.

ABOVE: The Garland King from Castleton, England, may represent the last memory of the ancient sacrifice of the Year King.

On the 29th of May the church bell rings at two o'clock to call the [people] *together to make a garland of Mayflowers and ginger-flowers* (wild geraniums). . . . *The framework of the garland is kept at the parish clerk's house, to be used every year. It is like a beehive in shape. On the top of it they fix a large bunch of choice flowers which they call "the queen" (locally pronounced "quane"). This bunch of flowers is fastened to a stick which fits into a round hole in the top of the garland frame. The garland itself is made chiefly of wild flowers. . . . There are people in Castleton who still grow tulips and other flowers for the garland, especially for "the queen."*

Before the garland is put on the king's head, the king and queen ride round the village, dressed in their costume, to "advertise themselves," and to show the people that the ceremony is about to begin. [Then] the garland is put over the king's head by two strong men, who stand on two barrels or stools. . . . The king then rides from one inn in the village to another, with the queen. . . . The garland covers him down to the hips, so that you can see nothing of him but his legs. His arms are inside the garland, steadying it. It is so heavy that it makes him sweat. . . . He is so encumbered by the garland that he cannot use the reins, and his horse has to be led. He can move aside some of the leaves . . . of the garland in order to see through.

The woman, lady, or queen taking part in this ceremony is a man dressed in woman's clothes. . . . The queen now wears a jewelled crown, bought a few years ago; formerly it was an old bonnet. . . .

After [the King and Queen] *have done riding round, the king rides alone into the churchyard. He sits on his horse, close to the south wall of the tower, when the ringers remove the nosegay called "the queen" from the top of the garland, and a rope is let down from the summit of the tower, put through the hole left by the removal of "the queen," and fastened inside by the king. Six or eight men are standing on the top of the tower; less than six could not manage it. The rope goes over a stone which projects from the leads of the tower, and serves for a pulley. The men pull the rope, the garland is lifted from the king's head, and raised to the top of the tower. It is then fixed "on the pike," ie. on the middlemost of the three pinnacles on the south side. (Folk-Lore, vol. 12, 1901).*

Here are the central characters of a far older ceremonial, the last echoes of a ritual in which the garlanded King, (remembered by local people to have been called simply "the man," as the Queen was also called "the woman") would have been sacrificed, and either his severed head or his entire body hauled up to the top of a tree.

A ROMAN FEAST

The date of the Castleton ceremony, May 29th, coincides with the ancient Roman feast of *Ambarvalia*, in which the god Mars, a god of agriculture before he was a god of war, was propitiated in order to ensure a good harvest. A typical prayer for this occasion begs "Father Mars"

> *. . . that thou mayest be propitious and of good will to me, our house and household, for which course I have offered the offering of a pig, sheep and ox to be led round my farm, that thou mayest prevent, ward off and avert disease, visible and invisible, barrenness and waste, accidents and bad weather, that thou wouldst suffer the crops and fruits of the earth, the vines and shrubs, to wax and prosper, that thou wouldst preserve the shepherds and their flocks in safety and give prosperity and health to me and our house and household. (J. C. Cooper, Aquarian Dictionary of Festivals)*

Interestingly, the offerings included flowers, posies, wreaths, and garlands—all emblems of greenness.

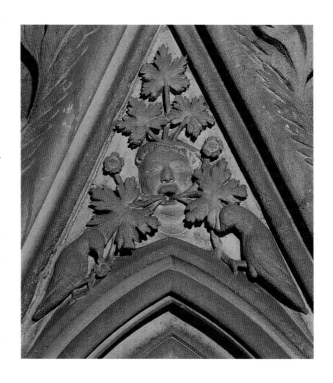

ABOVE: *The Green King from a tympanum arch in Southwell Minster, England, shows the skill of the thirteenth-century carvers.*

The presence of a significant number of Roman settlements in the area around Castleton suggests that the current ceremony may well have been influenced by Roman belief.

There may be echoes here too of another celebration, still acknowledged in Britain on this date by the wearing of green oak leaves. It is known as Oak Apple Day and probably once stood as a reminder of more ancient rites in which the oak was venerated. Banned in the seventeenth century during the rule of the Commonwealth, it was reinstated as part of the celebrations following the return of the monarchy in the person of King Charles II. As the story goes, during his escape from Cromwell's Roundhead soldiers, the king hid in an ancient oak. This is the official reason for the celebration of Oak Apple Day, but we may decry an older face peering at us from amid the leaves—that of the Green Man.

A similar ceremony to that of Castleton took place over Whitsuntide as late as the eighteenth century at

RIGHT: The face of the Spring Maiden depicted on an early fourteenth-century nave boss in Exeter Catherdral, England.

Grossvargula in Germany. Here, a figure known as "The Grass King" used to be led in a procession through the town. He was encased in a pyramid of poplar boughs, the top of which was adorned by a crown of flowers. The leafy pyramid covered both the man and the horse on which he rode, leaving only a small opening for his face. At the end of the day the Grass King was stripped of his green cover, the crown was given into the keeping of the mayor, and the branches were planted in the flax fields to encourage them to grow.

In each case, the object of these ceremonies is the same—to bring fruitfulness to the earth and ensure the health of the crops. That this once would have been attempted by human sacrifice is beyond question, as the story of the King of the Wood reminds us.

Much as we may rightly decry the practice of such sacrifice, it is an inherent part of the Green Man mythos. We will find, as we look deeper into his story, that many of the figures associated with the Green Man reflect his role as King of the Wood, and that the lives and deaths of his various later representatives parallel his own cyclic existence.

THE BATTLE FOR SPRING

Another figure is also present in the May Day rites. We know her best today as the Queen of the May. As we have seen, she was always a part of these ceremonies, functioning as the consort of the King of the Wood/Green Man, taking a new lover every year as her previous lord fell to the strength of his victorious challenger. Her presence in the Castleton ceremony, as well as in similar accounts from other parts of the country, draws attention to another important aspect of this tradition: an ancient ritual combat between the King of Winter and the King of Summer for the hand of the Spring Maiden.

This ancient mythic struggle appears in a number of traditional and literary sources with considerable

continuity. Its importance as a statement about the ritual year grew from the simple fact that if the Winter held the land in its grip for too long the planting of the crops might be delayed, with disastrous consequences. Thus the Champion of Summer must defeat the Champion of Winter, so that the Spring

Maiden might release the frost-bound earth and bring about the miracle of rebirth to the land.

This combat was still taking place well into the nineteenth century. As reported by Marie Trevelyan, this is how an aged Welshman described a staged ritual combat between Winter and Summer that took place in South Wales:

> When I was a boy, two companies of men and youths were formed. One had for its captain a man dressed in a long coat much trimmed with fur, and on his head a rough fur cap. He carried a stout stick of blackthorn and a kind of shield, on which were studded tufts of wool to represent snow. His companions wore caps and waistcoats of fur decorated with balls of white wool. These men were very bold, and in songs and verse proclaimed the virtues of Winter, who was their captain. The other company had for its leader a captain representing Summer. This man was dressed in a kind of white smock decorated with garlands of flowers and gay ribbons. On his head he wore a broad-brimmed hat trimmed with flowers and ribbons. In his hand he carried a willow-wand wreathed with spring flowers and tied with ribbons. All these men marched in procession, with their captain on horseback leading them, to an appropriate place. . . . There a mock encounter took place, the Winter company flinging straw and dry wood at their opponents, who used as their weapons birch branches, willow wands, and young ferns. A good deal of horseplay went on, but finally Summer gained the mastery over Winter. Then the victorious captain representing Summer selected a May King and the people nominated a May Queen, who were crowned and conducted into the village. (Marie Trevelyan, *Welsh Folk-Lore and Folk-Custom*)

The battle of the Summer and Winter Kings at one time would have ended in a ritual "marriage" between the victorious Summer King and his bride. By the time of the above account this practice would no longer have been sanctioned, hence we have here instead this more polite and acceptable version. As in the Castleton ceremony, the real nature of the celebration is hidden—though once again, it is only just beneath the surface.

LOVERS IN THE MAY

The May Day celebrations were notoriously licentious. Permission to cast off domesticity and unite in the greenwood came on Beltane Eve, when any girl could go to the forest and sleep with whomever she wanted. Most of the couples constituted in this way formed lasting, domestic relationships, and these

> The battle of the Summer and Winter Kings at one time would have ended in a ritual "marriage."

May Day frolics in the woods—merry-meet weddings in the groves—noticeably increased the population!

The characters of the May King and Queen reappear in a variety of stories and traditions from this time forward. For example, in the Robin Hood legends, which we will examine in detail in the next chapter, the outlaw and his May Day bride Marian celebrate their nuptuals and then flee the world for the sanctuary of the woods to live an idyllic life.

ABDUCTION OF THE FLOWER BRIDE

In some areas the May Queen or Spring Maiden is known as the Flower Bride, and in a variant version of the struggle between the Winter and Summer Champions she is abducted. To understand this abduction theme and the Flower Bride's role in the Green Man myths, we must turn to the romance

RIGHT: Queen Guinevere rides a-Maying in this Victorian painting by John Collier. She represents the Spring Maiden, whose fate is to be stolen away by the Lord of Winter.

literature of the Middle Ages, particularly the Arthurian legends. Here, we find this ancient myth preserved like a fly in amber.

In Sir Thomas Malory's fifteenth-century Arthurian romance, *Le Morte d'Arthur*, we find the following episode:

> *It befell in the month of May, Queen Guenever called unto her knights of the Table Round; and she gave them warning that early upon the morrow she would ride a-Maying in the woods and fields beside Westminster. And I warn you that there be none of you but that he be well horsed, and that ye all be clothed in green . . . and I shall bring with me ten ladies, and every knight shall have a lady behind him. . . . And so upon the morn they took their horses with the Queen, and rode a-Maying in woods and meadows as it pleased them, in great joy and delights.*

Into the midst of this idyllic scene, in which we notice immediately that the knights must be clothed in green, erupts the knight Meleagraunce, who has loved Guinevere from afar for years. He ambushes the party and carries off the Queen, imprisoning her in his tower. Lancelot, however, soon frees her after a hand-to-hand combat in which he finally slays the Queen's captor, Meleagraunce.

The true meaning of this story concerns the abduction of the May Queen, personified here by Guinevere. The earliest version, which also happens to be the oldest surviving example of an Arthurian story, appears carved in stone on the archivault of Modena cathedral in Italy. The first written version is contained in the twelfth-century *Life of Gildas* by Cradoc of Llancarven. He tells of how Guinevere was stolen away by Melwas (an earlier version of

Meleagraunce), King of the Summer Country, and imprisoned in the citadel of Glastonbury until Arthur laid siege to the place.

> *When he saw this, the abbot of Glastonia [Glastonbury], attended by the clergy and Gildas the Wise, stepped in between the contending armies, and in a peaceable manner advised his king, Melwas, to restore the ravished lady. Accordingly, she who was to be restored, was restored in peace and good will.*

Scholars have long recognized that this episode derives from the older mythic pattern of the struggle for the Spring Maiden, and, beyond this, from the ritual combat and death of the King of the Woods. Here Arthur takes the role of the Winter King to fight Melwas, King of the Summer Lands, for the hand of Guinevere, the Spring Maiden. The same story appears, even more clearly, in the following episode from "The Story of Culhwch and Olwen," in the medieval Welsh myth cycle known as *The Mabinogion*.

> *Creiddylad, the daughter of Lludd Llaw Ereint, and Gwythyr, the son of Greidawl, were betrothed. And before she had become his bride, Gwynn ap Nudd came and carried her away by force; and Gwythyr the son of Greidawl gathered his host together, and went to fight with Gwynn ap Nudd. But Gwynn overcame him. . . . When Arthur heard of this, he went to the North, and summoned Gwynn ap Nudd before him . . . and made peace between [him] and Gwythyr the son of Greidawl. And this was the peace that was made: that the maiden should remain in her father's house, without advantage to either of them, and that Gwynn ap Nudd and Gwythyr son of*

Greidawl should fight for her every first of May, from thenceforth until the day of doom, and that which ever of them should then be conqueror should have the maiden.

Interestingly, Gwynn ap Nudd, the adversary who steals Creiddylad, is a fairy being said to live beneath Glastonbury Tor, where in the previous story Melwas imprisons the maiden Guinevere. Creiddylad herself is elsewhere recognized as an ancient goddess of Spring.

So the struggle of the Lords of Summer and Winter, whether it be for Creiddylad, Guinevere, or the Queen of the May, is perennial—an enactment of the need to ensure the safe continuance of the seasonal round, something that was always in the minds of our ancestors. It was from their fear that the sun might one day fail to rise, or the corn to germinate, that myths of the sacrificed god first arose, and with them the embodiment of nature's own story in the characters of Green Man and the Flower Bride.

The question facing us today is: Is this indeed a match that will last "until doomsday"? In fact, we may now be capable of altering or perhaps even *ending* the seasons as we know them. Winds like el Nino now bring unseasonal rain to the deserts and drought to the fertile places as a result of global warming. Humanity can no longer lay safe bets on the spirits of the weather, nor be sure where the next meal is coming from, as fish, birds, and animals move from native habitats that we have ruined in search of food. Doomsday predictions loom nearer, perhaps, than ever before.

The liturgy on the following page from the United Nations Environmental Sabbath Project reminds us of our own urgent responsibilities and the need to return to the natural seasonal patterns we have already begun to disrupt.

ABOVE: Vexilla Regis by David Jones combines the symbolism of the Christian sacrifice with the wounding of nature today.

ABOVE RIGHT: The face of the Green Man in a carved roof boss from Sampford Courtnay, England.

We have forgotten who we are
We have alienated ourselves from the unfolding of the cosmos
We have become estranged from the movements of the earth
We have turned our backs on the cycles of life.

We have forgotten who we are

We have sought only our own security
We have exploited simply for our own ends
We have distorted our knowledge
We have abused our power.

We have forgotten who we are

Now the forests are dying
And the creatures are disappearing
And humans are despairing.

We have forgotten who we are

We ask forgiveness
We ask for the gift of remembering
We ask for the strength to change.

We have forgotten who we are

The earth will always need its champions, of whom the Green Man in his many guises is foremost. Can we number ourselves in the ranks of his supporters?

MEDITATION

THE GREEN LADY

Close your eyes and allow your present surroundings to fade into the background. In a moment you find yourself walking in an ancient woodland, with spring flowers opening at your feet and a delicious scent of May blossom in the air. Before you now is a soft green bank. Almost without thinking, you lie down and, breathing in the heavy scents of the blossom, drift gently into sleep.

In your imagination you are running through a deep part of the wood, where all sounds are hushed. You are impelled by an ancient longing—to be utterly free of all worldly pursuits and long-ings and to meet the primal beings who breath life into the forest. This desire gives you a strength and swiftness you have perhaps never known. The forest flies past on either side as you race onward!

The forest is dim and silent as you slow first to a trot, then a walk, and finally come to a halt, breathing in the stillness which must have existed before the first sounds were made.

Before you stands a tree of mighty proportions. You are about to approach it—drawn by some deep power you scarcely understand. Suddenly you see that it is no tree, but a giant green figure that towers above you, its back turned. Half in wonder and half in awe you are about to back away, when the figure begins to move.

The whole forest seems to hold its breath as the giant being slowly turns around. You see it is woman shaped, with skin that seems at once like bark and warm, breathing flesh. A wondrous cascade of hair falls about her shoulders and back. You are not sur-prised to see that it is as green as the ancient moss that grows everywhere in that place. And there, half hidden among the green tresses, tiny flowers

bloom—the white flowers of May that signal the coming of spring.

You find yourself regarded by two depthless eyes, wide and brown and shot through with silvery glints. Ancient eyes, deep, sorrowful, and joyous all at once. In your heart, suddenly, there grows a green spark. Warmth spreads through your whole body and thunders in your blood. You realize you are in the presence of the fount of life in all its multitudinous variety and burgeoning strength. Here is the Mother of All Living, the Green Lady of the Woods, who is also the Mountain Mother and the Mistress of the Sea. No words are spoken between you, but much is conveyed in the timeless moment between one breath and another. Every thought you have ever had is known to the Green Lady—good or bad—and is accepted—and understood—and changed in her green light. You are aware of many endings and many beginnings, things you have half-guessed in your dreams or deepest moments of waking realization.

Then the moment is over, and before you is only a great tree growing in the heart of the wildwood. But where before there was simply bare earth, a carpet of golden flowers has sprung up at your feet. You bend to touch one and a shiver of energy flows into you through your fingers. In your heart is the knowledge that you may pick one of these flowers for yourself . . . and this you do, placing it in your hair or through a buttonhole. The scent of myriad flowers comes from it.

You turn away reluctantly from that place and walk back through the forest until you come to the green bank where you see yourself still sleeping. Slipping back into your body is easy, and you begin slowly and unhurriedly to wake up.

Chapter Three

Gods of the Forest

Sherwood in the twilight, is Robin Hood awake?
Grey and ghostly shadows are gliding through the brake,
Shadows of the dappled deer, dreaming of the morn,
Dreaming of a shadowy man that winds a shadowy horn.

Alfred Noyes, *A Song of Sherwood*

The power of the trees and of the spirits of forest and woodland who guard them are everywhere around us when we enter one of the sacred groves of the world. There we feel close to the endless strength of creation, once again at one with the natural world that gives us life. Our ancestors saw the trees as bridges between earth and sky, as central points around which the heavens revolved. To walk in the woods today is to feel the echoes of those times and know for ourselves something of the timeless wisdom of the woods.

SACRED TREES

The Green Man comes to us out of the ancient forests and cannot be separated from the imagery of trees and woods. As we have seen, trees have always been considered sacred, even recognized as gods, by most ancient cultures. We find extensive tree lore especially among the Celts.

In medieval Irish the word for "sacred grove" is *fid-nemith* or *fid-neimid,* which in turn derived from an older Celtic word *nemetos*, meaning simply "holy" or "sacred." The tradition of the sacred grove or

ABOVE: The Druids held sacred groves of trees and stone circles.
RIGHT: Ancient trees were worshiped as "gods" of the forest.

nemeton was widespread throughout much of the western world. In Asia Minor in about 280 BC, the Gauls held a great council at a place called Drunemeton, "the chief nemeton or sacred place of the Druids." (Later, in Caesar's time, the Druids were said to meet annually in the land of the tribe known as the Carnutes, believed to lie at the exact center of Gaul and now generally accepted to be in the area of Paris.) We know that every tribe in Europe possessed such a *nemeton*, marked by a circle of trees or stones, and that such places were held in great awe. As the Roman military historian Tacitus says in his "Germania":

The grove is the centre of their [the Celts']* whole religion. It is regarded as the cradle of the race and the dwelling place of the supreme god to whom all things are subject and obedient.*

The Green Man, in whatever form he was then recognized, was this "supreme god," and our ancestors experienced his presence within certain trees.

The importance attached to specific trees in ancient Ireland is well documented in texts like the *Irish Triads*, complied in the Middle Ages from much earlier material. There we read:

Three noble, sacred things: groves or temples, filid or poets, and rulers. Three dead things that are paid for only with living things are an apple-tree, a hazel-bush, and a sacred grove.

This feeling is reflected in the harsh laws laid down for any damage caused to certain trees. In the early Irish law tracts called the "Senchas Mor," it is stated that the fines for cutting certain trees are as follows:

For the "Chieftain" trees: oak, hazel, holly, yew, ash, pine, and apple, the fine is a cow for cutting the trunks, a heifer for either limbs or branches. For the "Common" trees: alder, willow, hawthorn, mountain ash, birch, elm, and idha [possibly a species of pine], the fines are a cow for each whole tree and a heifer for the branches. . . .

And the list goes on. Each tree, just like a human being, has its honor price.

THE LORE OF TREES

The poetic writings of Ireland name five sacred trees: the Tree of Ross, the Tree of Mugna, the Tree of Dathi, the Tree of Usnach, and the Tree of Tortu. An early text, *The Calendar of Oengus*, recounts their history in poetic form:

> *Eo Mugna, great was the fair tree,*
> *high its top above the rest:*
> *thirty cubits—it was no trifle—*
> *that was the measure of its girth.*

> *Three hundred cubits was the height of the blameless tree,*
> *its shadow sheltered a thousand:*
> *in secrecy it remained in the north and east*
> *till the time of Conn of the Hundred Fights.*

> *A hundred score of warriors—no empty tale—*
> *along with ten hundred and forty*
> *would that tree shelter—it was a fierce struggle—*
> *till it was overthrown by the poets.*

ABOVE: The Norse world tree Yggdrasil gives life to the birds which feed on it in this medieval wood carving.

These enigmatic references suggest cosmic world trees of the kind worshiped among the Norse as representations of Yggdrasil, the World Ash. The ash, like the oak, was widely recognized as sacred, and it can hardly be accidental that three out of the five trees listed in the Irish poem belong to the ash's genus.

The fact that the great Oak of Mugna is described as being "overthrown by the poets" is puzzling at first. The poetic mysteries were intimately connected with tree lore, as we can see from the fact that the poets were the chief users of the sacred ogham alphabet, one form of which was based on a catalog of various species of tree.

But if the poets revered the sacred trees, why would they be described as destroying them? In the same text quoted above we learn of the fate of other mighty trees in terms that leave little room for doubt as to the answer:

> *How fell the bough of Dathi?*
> *It spent the strength of many a gentle hireling:*
> *an ash, the tree of the nimble hosts,*
> *its top bore no lasting yield.*
>
> *The Ash in Tortu—take count thereof!*
> *the Ash of populous Usnach:*
> *their boughs fell—it was not amiss—*
> *in the time of the sons of Aed Slane.*
>
> *The Oak of Mugna, it was a hallowed treasure;*
> *nine hundred bushels was its bountiful yield:*
> *it fell in Dairbre southward,*
> *across Mag Ailbe of the cruel combats.*
>
> *The Bole of Ross, a comely yew*
> *with abundance of broad timber,*
> *the tree without hollow or flaw,*
> *the stately bole, how did it fall?*

Cutting down these ancient trees, certainly the ones with Druid connections, seems to have been contemporaneous with the spread of Christianity and the ending of pagan ways. If we view the poets' deliberate cutting down of the trees in this light, we can conclude that they were trying to prevent their being felled by the axes of the monks.

This great respect for the power and sanctity of the trees, especially when they were part of a grove, is reflected throughout Celtic history and tradition and relates directly to the history of the Green Man. He too was cut down and driven into the darkest corners of the forest, until he returned to our awareness in the guise of the King of the Wood, the foliate heads, and the many other characters who bear the stamp of his archetypal presence.

ROBIN-I-THE-HOOD

We cannot go further in our examination of the Green Man without looking at the character of Robin Hood, whose story did much to promote a continuing knowledge of older forms of the Green Man among the Christianized people of England.

The main sources for Robin Hood's life are a series of popular ballads. Despite various unsuccessful attempts to date these or their sources, we can say they were well known by 1337, when the great religious poem of *Piers the Plowman* was written. In this poem the anonymous author writes:

> *I know not perfectly my pater-noster,*
> *As the priest would sing:*
> *But I know rhymes of Robin Hood,*
> *And Randolf Earl of Chester . . .*
> (John Matthews, trans.)

This poem makes it clear the Robin Hood ballads had already reached such a degree of familiarity that even a Christian cleric—who might not normally be supposed to be familiar with such things—knew them better than his prayers!

RIGHT: A contemporary Druid ceremony at Stonehenge honors the return of the life-giving sun. Many of the sacred ancient groves were destroyed when Christianity became widespread.

RIGHT: A Victorian illustration shows Robin at home in the Greenwood with some of his merry men.
BELOW: A chess set depicts the mythic characters of Sherwood.

In *The English and Scottish Popular Ballads*, Francis James Child lists four of the earliest ballads, probably dating from the fourteenth century. These ballads form the basis of the much longer *Little Gest* ["life"] *of Robin Hood*, which dates in its earliest printed form from 1492. By the time this work was committed to print, a large number of ballads featuring the famous outlaw were circulating widely. As the sixteenth-century historian John Mair remarks in his *History of Greater Britain* (1521):

> *The Feats of this Robin are told in song all over Britain. He would allow no woman to suffer injustice nor would he rob the poor, but rather enriched them from the plunder taken from abbots. The robberies of this man I condemn, but of all thieves he was the prince and the most gentle thief.*

This gives us an indication of the respect in which Robin was held. Even by those who could not outwardly condone his deeds, he was seen as essentially a good man, a prince among thieves, and a champion of the people. Moreover, he was acknowledged as the latest representative of the Green Man, being known among the common people as a green lord of the wildwood, a towering mythological figure who embodied the qualities of the King of the Wood and, later, the Lord of the May.

THE GOODLEY GEST
In a scene reminiscent of one in which the Round Table knights learn of their chivalric duties from

King Arthur, *The Little Gest* shows the merry men listening as their leader describes the proper way for them to behave:

> *Look you do no husband harm,*
> *That tilleth with his plough;*
> *No more you shall on good yeoman,*
> *That walked in Greenwood shawe;*
> *Nor no knight nor squire*
> *That would be a good fellow . . .*

Following this instruction, the outlaws offer help to a very poor knight named Sir Richard-at-Lee to recover money from the greedy Abbot of St. Mary's Abbey in York. But the author's attention quickly switches to the adventures of Robin's right-hand man Little John, who—under the assumed name of Reynold Greenleaf, another Green Man alias—enters an archery contest organized by the evil Sheriff of Nottingham.

Little John is so successful at his archery that the sheriff asks him if he would like to join his own soldiery. Little John agrees, as he had apparently intended to do in the first place.

Little John now follows a hunting party organized by the sheriff and, going by ways known only to those who live in the forest, soon overtakes them. When his surprised master asks where he has been, John answers:

> *I have been in this forest:*
> *A fair sight I can see:*
> *It was one of the fairest sights*
> *That ever yet saw I me.*
>
> *Yonder I saw a right fair hart,*
> *His colour is of green:*
> *Seven score of deer in herd,*
> *Be with him at bedene.*

On one level, this is simply Little John's cryptic way of referring to Robin and the outlaws, but on

ABOVE: Actor Kevin Costner plays Robin in The Prince of Thieves, *a modern version of the legend.*

an altogether deeper lever, he is describing Robin as a green stag with a herd of deer—terms applicable to an older time when he who wore the horns represented something else—the horned stag-god, the Green Man in his animal aspect, of whom we will have more to say shortly.

Little John leads the sheriff and his men straight to the outlaws camp, where they are at once imprisoned. The sheriff himself is stripped of his outer garments, wrapped in a green cloak, and then made to put on the green garb of the outlaws. He is then invited to a feast.

The next day Robin releases him on the promise that he will never harm any of the outlaws again—thus demonstrating that the outlaw was much more chivalrous than his opponent, who, of course, had no intention of honoring his promise.

THE DEATH OF THE FOREST LORD

After several more adventures the *Gest* ends with a brief reference to Robin's death at the hands of the Abbess of Kirklees. We have to turn to another ballad, "The Death of Robin Hood," for the end of the story. Even here the versions we have are curiously conflicting and fragmentary, and debate has centered on their real meaning. However, it is possible, with a little effort, to understand what is being said.

Growing old and ill Robin decides to visit his "kinswoman," the Abbess of Kirklees Priory near Peterborough, who is a famed healer. Apparently sensing trouble, Little John tries to persuade his master to take fifty men with him, but Robin refuses and in the end is accompanied only by John.

On the way they encounter a strange old woman beside a stream, who curses Robin. John is filled with foreboding but cannot persuade his master to turn back. At the Abbey John is locked out of the room where Robin is to be treated, and the Abbess begins to bleed her kinsman—a common treatment for most ailments at that time. However, as the ballad says:

ABOVE: On his deathbed, Robin Hood prepares to shoot his last arrow. Where it falls he will be buried.

> *And first it bled, the thick, thick blood,*
> *And afterwards the thin,*
> *And well then wits good Robin Hood*
> *treason there was within . . .*

With failing strength Robin blows his horn and Little John breaks in—too late to save his master. John begs to be allowed to burn Kirklees and all within it to the ground. But Robin rallies enough to say that he has never made war on women and will not begin now. He then begs to be helped to the window, and from there shoots his last arrow, declaring that he wishes to be buried where it falls. John carries out this duty and erects a stone above the grave bearing only the words: *Here lies bold Robin Hood.*

SACRIFICIAL BLOOD

Significantly, Robin's life ends by his bleeding to death—a ritual mode of human sacrifice in pre-Christian Europe. In the ballads, the Prioress is represented as an evil woman in league with an old enemy of Robin's, but it is much more likely that she represents the memory of the priestess of older times, whose task it was to let out the blood of the sacrificial King to fructify the earth.

In a variant version of the death ballad preserved in a thirteenth-century manuscript, we again encounter the old woman kneeling by a stream. She is apparently *banning* (that is, "cursing") Robin, and he asks her why. Unfortunately, the manuscript is fragmentary at this point and her answer is missing. Tantalizingly, the ballad takes up the story again after half a page:

> *. . . To give to Robin Hood;*
> *We weepen for his dear body,*
> *That this day must be let blood.*

Gods of the Forest **63**

This suggests that a number of people are weeping for Robin's impending death. Here it is likely that Robin *knows* that he is going to his appointed death and does so willingly.

The old woman at the stream is a variation of the bean sidhe (from which we get the word *banning*), a fairy woman also known as "The Washer-at-the-Ford." This hag-like woman was seen by Celtic warriors before a battle in which they were to die.

In this context, Robin is clearly a willing sacrifice. In fact, he is a representative of the King of the Wood, who must die in order that the seasons may continue to turn. Once, as we have seen, this sacrifice was a central part of the annual celebration of the dying and rising king. By the time of Robin Hood the Outlaw, in the thirteenth or fourteenth centuries, such things were no more than a memory, all but forgotten except in certain corners of the land such as Castleton and parts of Wales. Through the legends of Robin Hood the Green Man still reigned, but in a new form. Ever renewing like the greenwood he represented, he could change but not die!

THE REAL ROBIN

No adequate historical evidence exists to associate Robin Hood with any historical person or period before the emergence of the ballad as a literary genre. We may suppose that oral tales of the "Lord of Sherwood" were circulating before that time, but a whole series of events came together to create the character of Robin Hood as outlaw and as champion of the people. The time was right for the social injustice of land owners toward their tenants to become the setting for ballads. And if ancient pre-Christian traditions were still flourishing in many parts of the country, as seems likely, it was natural that the figure of the Green Man should reappear in a new guise that could be openly discussed and whose stories could become popular on the lips of the ballad

makers. Many folk traditions, including those surrounding the May Day games and dances, preserved elements that passed through the channel of the Robin Hood myths and emerged with new characteristics acquired from the ballads.

The fact that the emergence of Robin as a major character coincides with the proliferation of foliate heads is no accident. The relationship between the myths of the Green Man, the ballads of Robin Hood, and the folk traditions relating to May Day suggests that the forest god gradually developed into the outlaw of Sherwood, shedding certain characteristics and gaining others.

Traces remain in the celebration of the May Day games that hark back hundreds, even thousands, of years to another time and another culture in which the Green Man was honored as the spirit of Nature itself. We must look next at these celebrations to advance our understanding of the Green Man.

RIGHT: The Major Oak in Sherwood Forest is believed to be the traditional meeting place for Robin and his outlaws.

MEDITATION

THE GUARDIAN OF THE WOODS

Close your eyes and prepare to begin a journey to the heart of the wildwood. As your surroundings fade from consciousness you find yourself surrounded by towering trees. Their presences are as real as if you stood among a crowd of people. Yet they are not human. Their life force is deeper and more ancient than that of any human being. They are slow and thoughtful and they dream deeply the old thoughts of the earth.

Take time to wander though the forest. Look around you at the trees. See how many different kinds there are—oak, ash, thorn, willow, elm, beech, chestnut, apple, and pine. There are these and many more, for this is not merely a simple woodland where certain kinds of trees grow. It is *all* woodlands and combines within it all the different trees that grow in this land. Look at each of them and feel the one to which you are most drawn. Converse with it. Look at the shape of its leaves, the way the sunlight falls on its trunk, the dancing patterns made by the shadows of the leaves on the ground. Sit down and feel the depth of the loam beneath the trees, formed by countless years of fallen leaf mold. Lean back against the tree and let its thoughts become one with yours for a time.

When you are ready, get up and wander again through the wood. Listen now to the birdsong and the rustling of animals all around you. They too are part of the beating heart of the wildwood. Now let the song of the trees guide you through the thousand branching footpaths, past caves and bowers woven by the natural tracery of branches. Follow the way until you arrive in a sunny clearing where an ancient oak tree stands, a tree of such vast girth that it could offer shade for a hundred people. Ranged about the clearing are fallen logs, and you sit on one of them.

For a while you allow your thoughts to drift, unencumbered by the needs and worries of daily life. Here the peace of the timeless woods surrounds you, and you are truly at rest. Maybe you will see some of the figures to whom these woods are home: The King of the Wood, the Green Man, or Robin-i-the-Hood. Perhaps you will see them come out of the trees and join you in that quiet place, seating themselves on the fallen logs, speaking softly together or simply letting their thoughts drift as you are doing, in companionable silence.

After a time you become aware of a face looking out at you from the depths of the trees to one side. It is a face as brown and wrinkled as the bark of the trees themselves, but it is lit by a pair of the brightest eyes you have ever seen, eyes that understand all there is to understand—about human and animal and tree. The owner of the face steps shyly forth—a small figure, clad in a cloak of leaves and in clothes of tree bark. Long black hair tumbles about its face and you would be hard pressed to say what it gender is. Drawing near to you, it reaches out a long, twig-like hand and touches your brow for a moment. A tingling sensation speeds through you, leaving you with a sensation of inner warmth. No words are spoken, but much is conveyed.

You realize you are in the presence of an ancient spirit of the greenwood, so old that it no longer has a name, though it has had many in its time. It knows and remembers everyone who has ever walked in the woods—poets, dreamers, mystics, warriors, and kings—all who have ever come here in search of silence and wisdom. It has taught many to know the ways of this place and the mystery it guards in its heart, the mystery it will now show *you*!

Beckoning you to follow, the guardian leads you to one side of the clearing and in among the trees again. Here you see an ancient tree stump, older even than the great oak tree that stands guard at the center of the wood. This stump is all that remains of a tree that must have stood here when the first primal forest covered the world at the beginning of time. It has grown brittle with age and its heart is hollow. Here, as you look, you suddenly see a tiny spark of green-gold light. It grows swiftly until it is a bright fire glowing in the heart of the stump. From it comes such power as you may have never felt before. It is like bathing in the purest sunlight from which all harmful rays have been extracted. It is the pure golden light of the wildwood, the presence of which keeps it alive and brings those in search of wisdom to this place.

You stand entranced before the glowing heart of the forest until you have almost become part of it. You sense that if you remain here any longer you will start to become a tree yourself, to take root in the dreaming depths of the wood. Before that can happen, the ancient guardian touches your hand to remind you that it is time to leave. The green-gold glow dwindles to a tiny spark within the stump, and you follow your guide back to the clearing. As you do so you see animals and birds all around in the trees and bushes. They too have come to share in the magical power of the green-gold light.

At the clearing's edge the guardian bids you farewell and, in speech that has no words, conveys this message: You have walked in the heart of the wild-wood and have bathed in the light of its living force. Remember what you have felt, and whenever you pass a tree—whether it stands alone in a wilderness of human making or in the depth of woodland—pause and listen to its voice. For in many parts of the land the forests are dying. Only the hearts of those who have some of the true wisdom can save them.

As these words echo in your mind and heart, the forest begins to fade from around you and you awaken slowly to your normal consciousness. Yet the warmth of the forest's heart, its slow-breathing life force, and the words of the ancient guardian, remain with you. It is for you to see to it that the great tree-places of the world are not left to die or be cut down. For when the last tree falls, something of the utmost value will be lost forever from the created world, never to return. Ask yourself if you will allow that to happen!

Chapter Four

The Dancers in the Green

That man you saw-Lob-lie-by-the-fire, Jack Cade,
Jack Smith, Jack Moon, poor Jack of every trade,
Young Jack, or Old Jack, or Jack What d'ye call,
Jack in the hedge, or Robin Run by the Wall,
Robin Hood, Ragged Robin, Lazy Bob,
One of the Lords of No Man's Land, Good Lob—
Although he was seen dying at Waterloo,
Hastings, Agincourt, and Sedgemoor too—
Lives yet.

Edward Thomas

The sweet rich beauty of the earth is nowhere more apparent than during the spring, when everything seems more alive and the green energy of life flows through every tree and blade of grass. Into this land come the dancers who usher in the warm winds of summer, who celebrate the death and rebirth of the harvest fruits and the cyclically burgeoning life that is in everything and everyone. At this time the Green Man appears with all the elegant greenery of the reborn year. His energy is strong, youthful, eager. He invites us to join him in a dance to welcome the first shoots of grain, the unfurling leaves of forest and hedgerow.

THE MAY DAY REVELS

Throughout much of the Middle Ages, once the May blossom flowered, a kind of divine madness took possession of the people of Europe. Everyone, from kings to lowly commoners, took part in a variety of celebrations of the dawning spring, when the earth threw off the shackles of winter and new life appeared. The May Day games, or "revels," actually took place all through the summer, as well as on May 1, the date tradition said they should be held. Interestingly, from the 1500s until the end of the seventeenth century, they were almost continually ruled over by the figure of Robin Hood, to such an extent that these celebrations became known as "Robin Hood's Games."

Just as the introduction of the foliate heads into the gothic cathedrals of the Middle Ages represented the entrance into Christian architraves—by the back door—of the old pagan archetype of the Green Man as the spirit of nature, so these games represented the entrance of his wild forest energy into the ordered

ABOVE: The Green Man as personified by a modern "Mummer" at the Green Man festival held every year at Hastings, England.
RIGHT: The power of the greenwood shows itself in this vibrant aspen. The aspen was associated with death and the underworld.

realm of the secular city and everyday life. Wildness, of a kind deplored by so many Puritan writers that it must have had a strong hold on the imaginations of the people, broke out everywhere once the May Pole was erected.

These poles, most often of oak, elm, or birch, were brought from the forest and erected in town and village alike, where they became the focus of joyful, uninhibited games, feasting, and merriment. Significantly, May Day is the only survival of the ancient pagan festivals that does not have a Christian saint associated with it—a fact that probably explains both the continuing popularity of the May revels and the Church's opposition to them.

The May Pole harked back to the great world trees about which we learned in the previous chapter. It was an Axile Tree, connecting earth and heaven. The intertwining of the ribbons by the dancers echoed the intertwining of men and women at this joyous time of life's reaffirmation. As the people of village and town danced around the pole, winding themselves in intricate mazes of dance into the very heart of creation, they were, consciously or not, embodying a rhythm that has existed since the beginning of time and which is so clearly expressed in the procreative energy of the Green Man.

Many interpretations of the May Day games exist. We have already examined one of the most important of them—the battle between the Kings of Summer

TOP: The Green Man with his club is carefully watched by onlookers in this detail from a fifteenth-century painting.
ABOVE: A seventeenth-century painting portrays Morris Dancers on the banks of the River Thames near Richmond Palace, England.

RIGHT: *The half-green, half-white face of a Green Man from a modern troop of mummers, the Oyster Morris, from Canterbury.*

and Winter for the Spring Maiden. We can piece together a fairly complete picture of the meaning of these May Day celebrations from sources that show both the wide distribution of the revels and their deeper significance in terms of the ongoing story of the Green Man. Welsh folklorist Marie Trevelyan sets the scene beautifully:

On the morning of May Day—that is, at the very first glimmer of dawn—the youth and maidens in nearly every parish in Wales set out to the nearest woodlands. The gay procession consisted of men with horns and other instruments, which were played while vocalists sang the songs of May-time. When the merry party reached the woodlands each member broke a bough off a tree, and decorated the branch with flowers, unless they were already laden with May blossoms. A tall birch tree was cut down, and borne on a farm wagon drawn by oxen into the village. At sunrise the young people placed the branches of May beside the doors or in the windows of their houses. This was followed by the setting up of the May Pole on the village green. The pole was decorated with nosegays and garlands of flowers, interspersed with bright coloured ribbon bows, rosettes and streamers . . . the leader of the May dancers would advance to the pole, and tie a gay coloured ribbon around it. He was followed by all the dancers, each one approaching the pole and tying a ribbon around it until a certain number had been tied. The dance then began, each dancer taking his or her place according to the order in which the ribbons had been arranged around the pole. The dance continued without intermission until the party was tired, and then other dancers took their places.

Bringing in boughs clad with the new leafage of spring emphasized the people's desire to experience the joy of life.

The importance of these May Day celebrations was immense. Bringing in boughs clad with the new leafage of spring emphasized the people's desire to experience the joy of life through the greenery of spring and summer. That these festivals perpetuated the power of the Green Man in a nominally Christian world is evident.

GAMES OF MAY

One of the earliest reference to a festival that is similar in many respects to the Maytime events of the

Middle Ages, and which must have been wildly celebrated, is to be found in the *Chronicle of Britain*, written around 1155 by a Saxon priest named Layamon. He based his work on the earlier (1130) *History of the Kings of Britain* by Geoffrey of Monmouth. Geoffrey drew on still earlier documents, now lost, and on oral traditions dating back generations.

hundred thousand sheep, and all manner fowl at a number not lightly to be reckoned, besides thirty thousand in all of every sort of forest deer. And when they had paid all due honour unto the gods, they feasted them on the remainder . . . and the day and the night they spent in playing games of divers kinds.

. . . a celebration of the Celtic sun god Belenus, whom the Romans identified with Apollo.

Layamon elaborates:

ABOVE: *The "Paper Boys," a Morris team from Marshfield, in Gloucestershire, reenact the ancient death and resurrection play in which one of their number "dies" and is brought back to life.*

Geoffrey's account portrays a religious festival celebrating the Celtic king Cassivelaunus's defeat of Julius Caesar in c 53 AD. For this festival the barons of Britain and their wives were summoned to London to make offerings to their gods. Geoffrey writes:

They accordingly all came without tarrying and made sacrifice of divers kinds, and profuse slaying of cattle. Forty-thousand kine did they offer, a

The King began the rite after the heathen laws of the time. There were ten thousand men in the temple, the best of all Britons, standing before the mighty idol of Apollin. Each man held a torch, and each was clothed in gold, while the King wore a crown on his head. In front of the altar was a great fire set, and into this the King and all his greatest men cast gifts. . . . Thereafter they feasted on twelve thousand oxen, three thousand harts, three thousand hinds and countless fowl . . . then all the company repaired to the fields nearby, where they began to ride, and to run, and to play, while others fought with spear and shield, cast great stones, or played games on the table-board. (John Matthews, trans.)

The games described here by these two medieval authorities almost certainly refer to an annual celebration of the Celtic sun god Belenus, whom the Romans identified with Apollo, or "Apollin," so they seem to be memories of pre-Christian solsticial rituals and games.

By the thirteenth century there is abundant historical evidence of continuing games, sports, fairs and races held between May Day and Midsummer. That they were regarded as "dangerous" because of their pagan origin is made clear by the attacks mounted upon them by the Church, which even when it chose not to rely on accusations of heresy, fell back on three aspects of the revels they could easily attack: drunkenness, debauchery, and dancing—the last being thought of in the Middle Ages as an instrument of the devil that could easily lead to excessive behavior—particularly illicit sexual liaisons.

Nor were things to change much in the succeeding centuries. More than two hundred years later, in 1736, the minister of the deanery of Stowe in Gloucestershire issued a tract attacking the celebration of such games, which he declared "relics of paganism" and no more than thinly disguised echoes of "sacrificial worship."

They welcomed in the festival with loud blowing of horns . . . to drive away any fairies.

mountains and burned the gorse to frighten away the fairy folk. The next morning, they welcomed in the festival with loud blowing of horns, again to drive away any fairies who might be near. Then the May Queen rode a horse into the village, attended by some twenty maidens and an equal number of boys led by a captain who formed her bodyguard. Folklorist Eleanor Hull, quoting

ABOVE: *This sixteenth-century painting,* The Struggle of Carnival and Lent *by Pieter Brueghel the Elder, shows the Green Man accompanied by characters from the folk plays of the time.*

THE KING AND QUEEN OF MAY

The central figures of the games continued to be the Green Man and Green Lady, personified as the King and Queen of the May, just as they had been from the time of the King of the Wood and his bride.

We can see the extraordinary tenacity of these festivals from the fact that they have continued into the present. On the Isle of Man, as late as the 1920s, the festival of May Day was celebrated with full ritual panoply. On May Eve the people went into the

from a manuscript description of Manx customs, adds the following:

In opposition to her [the Queen of May] is the Queen of Winter, a man dressed in woman's clothes, with woollen hood, fur tippets, and laden with the heaviest and warmest habits, one upon the other. In the same manner are her attendants dressed, and she also has a captain and troop for her defence. Being

ABOVE: The Ravensbourne Men, *a contemporary painting by Carol Walklin, shows Morris dancers on the green.*

thus equipped as proper emblems, of the Beauty of Spring, and the Deformity of Winter, the two parties set forth from their respective quarters, the one preceded by violins and flutes, the other with the rough music of tongs and cleavers. Both parties march till they meet on a common, where their followers engage in a mock battle. If the forces of the Queen of Winter get the upper hand and succeed in taking the Queen of May prisoner, she has to be ransomed for a sum which will pay the expenses of the day; after which, Winter and her attendants retire to a barn to amuse themselves while the others remain on the green, dancing for a considerable time. They conclude the evening with a feast, the Queen at one table . . . the captain at another.

Once again we have the battle between Summer and Winter; here it is two queens who enact the struggle, even though, presumably to keep the polarity of male-female, one of them is played by a man. We note that one of the underlying themes of the May Day revels was fear of the fairy folk—which was, in fact, fear of the old gods of human sacrifice that the fairies represented.

We can see the repressed theme of human sacrifice represented in parts of Scotland to this day, where a Beltaine bannock (a kind of hard biscuit) is cooked and broken into equal pieces, one of which is smeared with ash until it is black. The pieces of ash are then placed in a bag and everyone pulls one out. The person who gets the blackened piece then has to jump through a bonfire—once, a "bonefire"—a symbolic reenactment of the ancient sacrifice. In an earlier time this may have been the way

the sacrifice was chosen, and he or she burned.

In Scotland the Beltaine Fire Society still holds an annual festival on April 30, in which the members recreate the Green Man's courtship of the Green Woman and his death and subsequent rebirth, while at Hastings in Sussex a festival dedicated to Green

ABOVE: A contemporary procession of the Green Man in Hastings. BELOW: Green Jack and his merry company parade through the streets of old London in this eighteenth-century illustration.

Jack takes place annually during the month of May. Indeed, throughout Europe, the May Day revels are still vigorously celebrated today, with the Green Man playing a central part in all of them. As we shall see later, the same is true of the Midwinter celebration of the solstice, which continues across much of the world. Honored at both of these high points in the ritual year, the energy of the Green Man reasserts itself at a deep and unforgettable level of our consciousness.

THE GREEN JACK

Another important figure appears at the May Day celebrations, known as the Green Jack, or Jack-in-the Green, or sometimes as John Barleycorn. Though his name changes from season to season, his identity is

timeless. He has been an essential part of the celebration of Maytime and Midsummer from early times and is still part of them today. Despite the age of this character, the earliest reference to him appears in *Sports and Pastimes of the People of England* by J. Strutt, published in 1801. Here the description of the May Day festival includes chimney sweeps.

> The trickster Robin Goodfellow often took the shape of a sooty chimney sweep to play his tricks on mortals.

Jack's connection to the chimney sweeps is interesting for several reasons. To this day in parts of Britain, the sweeps are associated with good luck and so are often invited to weddings. The motive may go back as far as Celtic tradition, where black or "sooty" characters were thought of as powerful and otherworldly, related perhaps to the ancient smith gods who were believed to be especially potent. The trickster Robin Goodfellow, whom we met earlier, often took the shape of a sweep to play his tricks on mortals.

The symbolism here suggests that those who enter the Underworld and return, retain for a while the dark color attributed to that place. Of course, the sweeps were also associated with ashes—and hence, like the Beltain bannock, were a reminder of the ancient sacrificial burnings. The ashes from such burnings were believed to be a fertilizing element and potent, like the smith gods who symbolized the transforming, life-giving power of the "refiner's fire."

RIGHT: The Straw Bear led through the streets of Whittlesea celebrates the successful harvest.

Strutt's description suggests that the presence of the Jack in these celebrations was familiar both to the writer and to the people. He writes:

> Some of the larger companies [of Sweeps] *have a fiddler with them, and a Jack-in-the-Green, as well as a Lord and Lady of the May, who follow the minstrels in great stateliness, and dance as occasion requires. The Jack-in-the-Green is a piece of pageantry consisting of a hollow frame of wood or wicker-work, made in the form of a sugarloaf, but open at the bottom, and sufficiently large to receive a man. The frame is covered with green leaves and bunches of flowers interwoven with each other, so that the man within may be completely concealed, who dances with his companions.*

The mention of the Jack's presence in the sweep's entourage is reminiscent of the description of the Castleton Garland Day figure, who harks back to even older archetypes of the Green Man.

THE LIFE OF THE CORN

The variety of ways in which the Jack appears in these festivals makes it difficult to arrive at a really clear picture of him. But one of the names associated with him offers an important clue. This is the Corn King, or "John Barleycorn" as he is known in England. We have met him before (in the prelude, page 11).

This ancient figure is found wherever the growing of grain is central to the survival of the people. Indeed, the yearly cycle of the corn—its planting, growth, and cutting down, followed by the repetition of this whole process—establishes it as a suitable metaphor for the cyclical nature of life itself. Particularly among those cultures that believe in reincarnation, it is possible to see the "life" of the corn as a potent echo of human existence, which also draws its strength from the earth. In ancient times the earth was thought of as the Mother of all living things, she who gave life and received it back again—through the interment of human remains, through blood sacrifice, through the ritual spilling of human seed upon the earth, and through the yearly replanting of the corn.

The traditional English folksong quoted on page 11 sums up this idea. Though men plough the corn into

ABOVE: A Morris group at Thaxted enact the age-old battle between Winter and Summer in Oxford.
LEFT: The Green Man appears out of the vine leaves at Southwell Minster, England. This carving dates to c. 1290.

the earth, and cut it down at harvest time, it shoots up again every spring. From the corn comes bread—essential for the continuance of human life—and, when brewed, beer. Like the Green Man, John Barleycorn (whose name means "the heart of the barley") would not lie down. The many figures dressed in straw who accompany Green Jack, or sometimes take his place in the revels, show how much the vitality of the Corn King is still recognized, even though few now know the true nature of his role in the Green Man's yearly cycle.

THE OLDEST DANCE

Green Jack also became an important character in the famous Morris dances performed over much of Europe, many of which continue today. These are generally enacted by groups of local people, often families who have kept alive the traditions for generations. Involving a team of varying numbers of men (and, rarely, women), the dancers carry sticks or kerchiefs and dance a broad variety of complex steps to the accompaniment of fiddle or accordion.

The name "Morris" may derive from the term "Moor" and originally refer to the fact that the dancers blacken their faces. Whether or not this blackening of the faces ever referred to the dark-skinned Moors of northern Africa, it certainly carries associations with the black-faced chimney sweeps and ancient smith gods, and, through them, with the spirits of the Otherworld, including the victims of sacrificial burning.

The "fairies" are beautifully dressed in ribbons and bells that glitter in the sun; the "animal men" are roughly clad in skins.

The Morris dance may have originated in Eastern Europe, an idea supported by the description of a dance still current in Romania. Here the dancers are called *Calusari,* a name often translated as "fairies" or "little horses." This remarkable dance consists of a kind of contest between the "fairies" and "the animal men." The former are beautifully dressed in ribbons and bells that glitter in the sun; the latter are roughly clad in animal skins and carry a short (phallic?) May Pole, garlanded with wild garlic. Beginning early in the morning, the whole team goes through a kind of initiation rite in which each man is beaten with staves. Then a ring is formed by the "fairies" in which a symbolic wedding ceremony takes place, occasionally interrupted by the "animal men" who attempt to push their way "into the house." Finally, women bring out any sick children in the village and the "fairies" dance around them. The whole day ends in a

ABOVE: The ancient fertility symbol of the "oss" in Thaxted during a yearly celebration of the folk-dance traditions of Britain.

public dance. Girls who manage to touch one of the dancers are assured of fertility and a happy marriage.

This festival clearly derives from a far more ancient ceremony, one that shares enough features with the Morris dance to suggest a connection. The dance in which a symbolic wedding is interrupted by animal men points to a time when the village shaman would have performed a healing dance around his patients.

The connection with horses, symbols of animal virility, leads us to the presence of another character

RIGHT: The burr-covered Burryman brings good fortune to the people of South Queensferry on the Firth of Forth, Scotland.
BELOW: The Abbots Bromley Horn Dance echoes a pre-Christian ceremony, when men were closer to the world of animals.

in the dances—the Hobby Horse or "Oss"—an embodiment of the Green Man's animalistic sexual prowess and fertility. We can still see the Oss at many performances where Morris dancing takes place. The Oss is usually a man dressed in a strange costume that includes a horse-skull mask, a wide hooped skirt, and sometimes a hobbyhorse stick with mask or skull attached.

This strange and sometimes sinister character plays tricks on people and chases them—especially young women, whom he covers with his wide skirt in order to confer his "blessing" upon them. The Oss who takes part in the Padstow May Day celebrations wears a hoop daubed with tar; the women he "blesses" are marked with black smudges.

THE FURRY DANCE

One of the oldest and best established celebrations involving Morris dancers takes place at Helston in Cornwall on May 8 every year. It has been celebrated in much the same way for several hundred years and is known as the Furry Day, or more recently, Floral Day. This festival preserves one of the most powerful traditions relating to the Green Man.

The following description, from *The Gentleman's Magazine* for June 1790, is intriguing.

In the morning, very early, some troublesome rogues go round the streets with drums, or other noisy

instruments, disturbing their sober neighbours, and singing parts of a song [in which there is mention] of going to the green wood to bring home "the Summer and the May-O." And, accordingly, hawthorn flowering branches are worn in the hats. The commonality make it a general holiday; and if they find any person at work, make him ride on a pole, carried on men's shoulders, to the river, over which he is to leap in a wide place, if he can; if he cannot he must leap in, for leap he must, or pay money. . . . About the middle of the day they collect together, to dance hand-in-hand round the streets, to the sound of a fiddle, playing a particular tune, which they continue to do until it is dark.

This sounds like the May Day games described above. But there are some interesting variations, such as the enforced leaping over a pole laid across the river. This theme is reminiscent of the first meeting between Robin Hood and Little John, when they engaged in just such a combat at a ford. On one level, this seemingly innocent encounter can be seen as no more than "horse play." On another, it echoes an age-old combat in which two men met at a ford and fought to the death, the victor taking the role of the man he slew. It is, of course, the same story as the ancient struggle of the Year King or the King of the Wood, and it resonates with another contest—that of the struggle for the Maiden of Spring. The song referred to in this account takes us back into Robin Hood territory:

> *Robin Hood and Little John.*
> *They both are gone to the fair,*
> *And we'll go to the merry green wood,*
> *To see what they do there.*
> *For we were up as soon as any day*
> *For to fetch the summer home,*
> *The summer and the May, O,*
> *For the summer now is come!*

RIGHT: The May Day celebrations were banned by the Puritans but were triumphantly restored during the reign of Charles II.

The meaning of this song is clear enough—Robin and John have gone to the greenwood to fetch home the summer—i.e., they have gone to bring home the bride of the May in the guise of Maid Marian.

The name of the ceremony—"Furry Dance"—may derive from "Flora's Dance," an ancient Roman festival in honor of Flora, the goddess of spring and summer. But a more obvious derivation suggests itself: the dancers of Helston are really dancing a "fairy dance" much like the Romanian fairy dances. In that case, they are following the footsteps of those otherworldly beings who, some still believe, leave rings of trodden wheat throughout the countryside.

THE FATE OF THE GAMES

By Tudor times, in the face of the Church's continued opposition, the object of the games had declined to such an extent that they were concerned only with the collection of money for the parish. Troops of people led by a Robin Hood impersonator rode from village to village, performing a play accompanied by a minstrel and two drummers. Although these fleeting manifestations continued in desultory fashion as late as 1607 in England and 1610 in Scotland, they were underground springs by then, their players subject to fine or even excommunication if caught.

In some places attempts were made to stop the games altogether. They were officially banned in

ABOVE: A "green" cross decorates Charlton on Otmore Church during May Day celebrations.

May Day celebrations helped keep alive the sacred power of the Green Man and Green Lady in hearts and souls.

Scotland in 1555; but when attempts were made to enforce the law, rioting broke out. In 1580, Edmund Asshton described the May Day rites as "lewde sports, tending to no other end but to stir up our frail natures to wantoness." In *The Anatomy of Abuses,*

published in 1585, Phillip Stubbs similarly condemns the May Day celebrations:

Against May, every parish, town, and village, assemble themselves together, both men, women and children, old and young . . . and either going all together, or dividing themselves into companies, they go some to the woods and groves, some to the hills and mountains, some to one place, some to another, where they spend all the night in pastimes, and in the morning they return, bringing with them birch, bows, and branches of trees to deck their assemblies. . . . I have heard it credibly reported . . . that of forty, threescore, or a hundred maids going to the wood over night, there have scarcely the third part of them returned home again undefiled.

Reading between the lines, we can hear more than just disgust at these "heathenish practices" being expressed. Fear seems to be present as well—fear about the loss of control some people believed inevitably followed such uninhibited festivals celebrating half-remembered deities of the pre-civilized past. What appeared as unbridled lust to the puritanical mind was, in fact, the energy of nature let loose to roam and ravage as it willed. The freedom of spirit and the joyous simplicity of life expressed in the May Day games represented everything the Puritans tried to outlaw and proscribe.

All the repressed energies of sexuality, bawdiness, and love of life suppressed by the gloomy Puritans broke out in riotous abandon once Charles II was on the throne. In a statute dating from shortly after his return, he commanded that:

> *for his good people's recreation, after the end of Divine Service, his good people be not disturbed . . . or discouraged from any lawful recreation; such as dancing, flirtation: either men or women; archery for men, leaping, vaulting, or any other such harmless recreation; nor from having any May Games, Witson Ales, and Morris Dances, and the setting up of May Poles, and other sports therewith used.*

It was at this point, as we saw earlier, that Oak Apple Day began to be celebrated, acknowledging in an only half-understood way the restoration of the Green Man under the relaxed reign of the "Merry Monarch."

THE MEANING OF THE MAY

Under the sunny skies of "Merry England" the May Day celebrations helped keep alive the sacred power of the Green Man and Green Lady in the hearts and souls of the Christianized people of England.

Embodied in the games, the mysteries of the May King and Queen, the struggle between the Kings of Summer and Winter, and the death and resurrection of the Corn King were ever present.

To this day in the May Day revels and celebrations, unofficial paganism exists side-by-side with official Christianity, and the merry Morris dancers preserve the light of a more ancient culture that attempted to recreate an earthly paradise in which the powers of the earth and of fertility met and conjoined. The law of the Green Man and his consort the Green Lady still flourishes, for a time at least, when the May Pole, connecting earth and heaven, winds those who dance about it into the endless pattern of creation, making

RIGHT: Hyman, here played by Leder Hawkins in the New Globe production of As You Like It, *represents the presence of green youth in the midst of hoary old age.*

ABOVE: Robin Hood is commemorated in this stained glass panel. He has an established association with the May revels.
RIGHT: Mary Fedden's illustration for the book The Green Man *by Jane Gardham. The shadow of the devil can be seen in the foreground as he tries to tempt the Green Man to betray earth.*

them one with the god and goddess. The human representatives of the May King are no longer killed, for obvious reasons, but the dance still remembers and honors the original sacrifices, long after most have forgotten the games' true meaning.

In this chapter we have moved from the bright gateway of spring to the deeper door of summer, where the Green Man takes upon himself the richer colors of the season. He is at his strongest here, bursting with life and energy, inviting us to celebrate summer's bounty, to join him in a dance that embodies the fecundity of the earth, the blossom-weighted boughs, and the high green shafts of the ripening corn. Ahead lie the challenges of autumn and winter, when new and different figures come knocking at the door.

MEDITATION

A VISION OF THE MAY

Prepare to embark upon a journey to another time and place. Close your eyes and let your surroundings fade, to be replaced by another scene.

You are standing on top of a range of low hills overlooking a mighty forest that stretches below you like a vast green sea. Its extent is far greater than any forest known to this world. It is the wildwood, where you will journey in search of wonder and wisdom and hear the song of the wild places.

From far away on the wind's breath, now comes the sound of music, and suddenly you see coming from the distance along the ridge of hills a party of merry folk. Their voices are raised in song and they dance along the way. They are carrying a huge pole, decked with flowers and ribbons. Behind the pole bearers streams the rest of the party, singing and dancing to the music of pipe, drum, and tabor.

As they come closer, they invite you to join them. Your feet take up the rhythm of the dance and you are carried irresistibly in their wake, down the hillside and into the vast reaches of the wildwood.

Soon the paths open out into wide meadows by the side of a swift flowing river. Here the revelers set up the mighty pole, and as each person takes a ribbon in his or her hands they weave an intricate pattern around and around the axis of the pole.

As you watch, you realize that the pole has grown somehow larger. Its flower-bedecked head now towers into the sky, and above it you see a faint gleam of stars. The ribbons too have grown longer, and as the dancers turn, they seem to float above the earth, their flying feet and whirling garments spiraling out in a dazzling rainbow of color. As the dance reaches a crescendo you hear a distant horn call echoing amid the trees, and as you turn you see another group of dancers, led by a tall figure who carries a long bow and wears a hood of green; Robin Hood himself now joins the dance! Now you cannot keep from dancing too!

Again you hear a horn, and everyone falls silent, turning toward the wood. You see a lone figure approaching, dressed in pure white, with white flowers in her long hair. Where she walks, white and golden flowers spring up. From her hands trail long ribbons of blossom, and in her face is a dream of spring that moves your heart and soul.

Thus does Marian come to join the dance. As Robin steps forward to take her hand, a cheer goes up from the crowd. The Lord and Lady of the Wildwood approach the great may pole and begin to dance alone, a slow and stately measure. As you watch in wonder the pole slowly begins to change, until it is no longer a bare pole, but has become a tree in the fullness of its growth, a tree decked with ribbons of blossom and leaf.

Winding gently inward to the center, Robin and Marian finally come together at the foot of the tree and exchange a kiss. The revelers cheer again to a loud blowing of horns.

Silence falls. Then with a sudden rush of wings a great flock of white birds flies down and settles on the branches of the May tree. Their song fills your head, and as the scene slowly begins to spin and dissolve, you catch a glimpse of the birds descending to form a circle of white around the Lord and Lady of the Wood.

You awaken to find yourself back in your own time and place, but with a feeling of peace and joyousness that grows deeper as you rise and return to the outer world.

Chapter Five

The Green Gome

Come, as the Green Knight to Gawain at the beginning
of the new year—
out of his oaken crevice:
ihude sing cuccu!

Ronald Johnson, *The Book of the Green Man*

As we enter this new curve of the Green Man's year we find ourselves in a darker landscape, where winter etches harsher outlines upon the land. In this place the Green Man is more cruel; rather than leading us in the merry dances of spring, or the celebrations of summer, he becomes a challenger, demanding that we find the courage to face the harsher realities of life. No less vigorous than his old self, this new aspect of the Green Man invites us to dance again. But now the steps are different, leading us into a darker place where we must acknowledge the presence of death.

A CHALLENGER AT THE GATE

In the fourteenth century, just as some of the finest foliate heads were being carved, a poem appeared about the tests and trials of the Green Man—a poem of such strength and beauty that it has remained essential reading for all who love the Arthurian mythos, or who love poetry for its own sake. Written

ABOVE: This Green Knight from Winchester Cathedral is roughly contemporary with the poem Sir Gawain *and* The Green Knight.
RIGHT: The fearsome Green Knight's cave at Wetton Mill is still believed to have been the home of the green gome.

somewhere in the area of Cumbria, it is called *Sir Gawain and the Green Gome*. We know it better as *Gawain and the Green Knight*. The story it tells is of an adventure that begins at Christmastide in Camelot.

Just as Arthur and his knights and their ladies are sitting down to dinner, they hear a loud crash of thunder, and into the hall rides a terrifying figure.

From his neck to his loins so square set was he, and so long and stalwart of limb, that I trow he was half a giant. And yet he was a man, and the merriest that might ride. His body in back and breast was strong, his belly and waist were very small, and all his features full clean.

> *Great wonder of the knight*
> *Folk had in hall, I ween,*
> *Full fierce he was to sight,*
> *And all over bright green.*

This powerful and threatening figure offers to play "a Christmas game" in which he will exchange blows with any man there, on condition that whoever gives the blow will accept a blow in return. Gawain alone has the courage to face the giant, and with the Green Knight's own ax cuts off his head. To everyone's

ABOVE: The hero Gawain sets out on a journey in this Dutch medieval illustration from the poem Walewain.

THE DEADLY GAME

In this first part of the poem, the Green Knight comes with an offer: to play a game in which he will allow himself to be sacrificed—his head severed from his neck—if his opponent will submit to the same test in a year's time. This kind of exchange reflects an ancient concept at the heart of the Green Man's story. As the guardian of the natural world, he

> As the guardian of the natural world, he challenges us to honor the sacrifice he makes every winter.

challenges us to honor the sacrifice he makes every winter—by making our own self-sacrifices of love, trust, and service to created things.

The Green Knight himself is a representative of both winter and of the vegetative world, as we know by his coloring and appearance, announced by thunder, at the Christmas court. He represents the winter aspect of the Green Man at his most terrifying in holding the power of the death that leads to renewed life over the one who accepts his challenge, demanding of Gawain the same courage demanded of us when we undertake a task that seems too frightening or difficult. This theme is what makes the poem at once powerful and exciting; we recognize something of ourselves in Gawain and follow his response to the Green Knight's game with a mixture of wonder and apprehension.

A FOOTSTEP IN THE CHAMBER

The second part of the poem tells of the turning of the seasons and of Gawain's approach to his terrible challenge. He sets out in search of the Green Chapel, and finally arrives at a castle, that of Sir Bercilak, a fierce and hearty lord. Sir Bercilak tells Gawain that the place he is seeking lies close at hand, and he offers

horror, the monstrous visitor does not fall. Instead, he rises, takes up his head, and holds it aloft! The lips move and the voice speaks, telling Gawain that he must journey to the Green Chapel and in one year receive in return the same blow he has struck. The Green Knight then mounts his horse and rides from the court, leaving everyone stunned and Gawain wondering what exactly he has promised.

ABOVE: The Green Knight plays the Beheading Game in this illustration from the poem Sir Gawain and the Green Knight. *RIGHT:* The Green Gome, *a modern woodcut by Bill Lewis.*

the knight hospitality and the services of a guide when the day of the trial comes.

Gawain accepts the offer and settles down to enjoy the hospitality of his host. Every day Bercilak leaves the castle to hunt, returning with various animals he has killed. Each time, before leaving, he proposes an exchange: He will give Gawain whatever he kills in the hunt in return for whatever prize Gawain wins at home. Gawain agrees, expecting to win nothing. But Bercilak's beautiful wife intends otherwise. Every morning, as soon as her husband has departed, Lady Bercilak enters Gawain's bedroom and offers herself to him. Gawain, reknowned throughout Arthurian tradition as a famous lover but here described as the soul of chivalry and courtesy, refuses all but a chaste kiss, which he faithfully awards to Sir Bercilak when he returns.

This curious exchange is repeated three times; each time, Gawain, fearing the inevitability of his death at the hands of the Green Knight, finds it harder and harder to refuse the lady. At last she persuades him to accept a gift—a green baldric that she tells him will protect him from the death he fears. Finally, the day dawns when he must make his way to the Green Chapel. As promised, Bercilak provides a guide, and soon Gawain finds himself in a strange place. The poem describes it this way:

> *At length a little way off he caught sight of a round hillock by the side of a brook, and there was a ford across the brook, and the water therein bubbled as though it had been boiling. The knight . . . walked round about it, debating within himself what place it might be. It had a hole at the end and on either side, it was overgrown with tufts of grass and was all round and hollow within. . . .*

The Green Knight now appears, and Gawain kneels to receive the blow. Twice his adversary feints, then mocks Gawain's courage. Finally, he nicks Gawain's neck and declares himself satisfied. To Gawain's astonishment and wonder the Green Knight reveals that he is, in fact, Sir Bercilak, and that the enchantress Morgane has put him and his wife under a spell. (Actually, Gawain had already seen Morgane in the castle disguised as an ugly old woman.) Morgane set up the whole business to test the courage of Arthur's court, and Gawain's in particular. The only reason for Gawain's slight neck wound is that he failed the test at the last minute by accepting Lady Bercilak's gift of the green baldric because he thought it would protect him.

THE RIDDLE ANSWERED

We learn at this point that the whole latter half of the poem is a further test—a restatement, in even more human terms, of the Green Knight's challenge, which is about finding true courage and of knowing how to act in the face of adversity. So, one of the gifts of the

Green Man is that he instructs us in how to face our deepest fears and conquer them. In this way he becomes a companion as well as a challenger, a dual role that is present in the archetype in virtually all of its manifestations. Whether aiding in the life-affirming celebrations of May, or offering a way back to a once acknowledged connection with the natural world in other ways, the Green Man draws us ever more deeply into the magical pattern of the year. In doing so, he also encourages us to realign our own lives with the rhythms of nature and to experience our own personal life stories as journeys of challenge, self-sacrifice, death, and rebirth.

CUROI AND THE BACHLACH

Behind the alternately charming and sinister figures of Bercilak and the Green Knight lies a figure from Celtic myth—Curoi Mac Daire. This character is a mixture of historical personage and mythic

being. He was probably a real king of Munster in Ireland, sometime during the Heroic period (roughly equivalent to the Bronze and Iron ages), but he is best known through the saga that celebrates the life of the more famous Irish hero, Cuchulainn.

Curoi's otherworldly nature is revealed in the medieval Irish tale *Fled Bricriu* ("Bricriu's Feast"), which has long been recognized as a primary source for *Gawain and the Green Knight*. In this story Curoi appears at a feast in the shape of a giant, who offers to play the Beheading Game with not one but three heroes: Conall Cearnach, Laoghaire, and

LEFT: A medieval carving from Sibton Church, Suffolk, England, shows the Bachlach holding a club.

ABOVE: The challenging face of the Green Man looks out from these two roof boss carvings from Sampford Courtenay, Devon.

Cuchulainn. The object of the game is to establish which of the three will be the supreme champion of all Ireland. The game consists of each of the heroes being allowed to cut off Curoi's head—in return for allowing him to do the same to them. Expecting no retaliation, both Laoghaire and Conall Caernach strike their blows, but in each case Curoi replaces his head after the blow.

At this terrifying event Conall Caernach and Laoghaire flee. Cuchulainn alone is prepared to accept the return blow. But when it comes, the giant only grazes the hero's neck with the blunt edge of the ax. He then declares Cuchulainn to be the bravest

man in Ireland, saying, "The sovereignty of the warriors of Ireland to you from this hour, and the champion's portion without dispute, and to your wife precedence over the women of Ulster forever." Then he departs. Only later is it revealed that he was Curoi in disguise, come to test the courage of the heroes and the worthiness of Cuchulainn in particular.

The same story appears in one other place, a tale called *The Tragic Death of Curoi Mac Daire*. In this story, the fairy woman Blathnat is one of the spoils of a siege in which the warrior Curoi had fought bravely, but in disguise. Because no one knew who he was, he received none of the fruits of battle. This injustice made him so angry that he seized Blathnat, two magical cows, and three birds that perched in their ears, causing them to give milk thirty times that of a normal animal. Putting the birds into his belt, and holding Blathnat under one arm and the cows under the other, Curoi fled. Cuchulainn chased and fought him, but was defeated. Curoi shaved Cuchulainn's head, buried him up to his armpits in mud, and covered him with cow dung. Cuchulainn was so angry that once he got free he followed Curoi and, discovering his true identity, planned his death with the help of Blathnat, who by now was Cuchulainn's lover. Blathnat bound Curoi to the bed by his hair, and Cuchulainn burst in and cut off his head.

ANOTHER GREEN GIANT

We can easily see that the story of Curoi's tragic death is yet another that follows the pattern laid out by the Green Man's yearly cycle. For example, it is strongly reminiscent of the abduction story we heard in chapter 2, where Guinevere is carried off by Meleagraunce. Here Curoi takes the place of Meleagraunce as the abductor, and Blathnat replaces Guinevere as the victim. The method of Curoi's death refers us back to the Beheading Game, though this time, since Curoi is unable to restore his severed head, Cuculainn is the winner of the contest.

In the ancient pattern, a fearsome creature of otherworldly origin comes to challenge a human hero to play the Beheading Game.

One of the most interesting details to emerge from comparing the stories of *Bricriu's Feast* and *Gawain and the Green Knight* is the use of a particular epithet to describe the rather fearsome giant in the former. This word is bachlach (pronounced "bachelach"). The similarity of this word to the name "Bercilak" immediately invites identifying the giant bachlach with the Green Knight.

In both cases the pattern is the same: a fearsome creature of otherworldly origin comes to challenge a hero to play the Beheading Game; the period of the challenge is for one year; and the object (hidden in the Gawain poem but still discernible) is the winning of the Spring Maiden. Bercilak is to Gawain as Curoi is to Cuchulainn. In each instance, representatives of the human world are challenged and tested by figures who can be considered otherworldly representatives of the Green Man.

THE GUARDIAN OF SUMMER

Another figure who deserves mention at this point is one who, together with his consort, stands as a guardian of summer in much the same way that the Green Knight is a guardian of winter. This strange being is known as Gromer Somer Jour, which means "Man of the Summer's Day," a name that makes his archetypal identity explicit. He appears in an extraordinary medieval poem called *The Wedding of Sir Gawain and Dame Ragnall*.

The story goes like this: While out hunting, King Arthur encounters a fierce and terrible adversary (Gromer) who, having separated the king from his

ABOVE: The face of the Green Knight from a fourteenth-century carving in the choir stalls of Bamberg Cathedral, Germany.
RIGHT: This contemporary image by Jane Brideson shows the dual nature of the Green Man, who can be both friendly and fierce.

companions, threatens to kill him. When Arthur asks for an opportunity to save himself, Gromer agrees only on the condition that Arthur finds within a year the answer to the riddle, What is it that women most desire? Agreeing to this bargain Arthur returns to court and asks his nephew Gawain to help him find the answer.

Both men now set out on a year-long journey, asking every woman they meet what it is that women most desire, and compiling a book of the answers, until finally the time is up. As Arthur sets off in despair to find Gromer, he meets a hideously ugly woman at the crossroads who offers to tell him the one true answer. But again, there's a condition: that she be allowed to marry Gawain—the handsomest, most desirable knight in all the land!

Sadly agreeing, Arthur continues on his way and gives Gromer the book of answers, hoping they will suffice. Only after Gromer rejects them all does the

identical to the Morgane we encountered in *Sir Gawain and the Green Knight.*

But the spell is not completely broken. Gawain has another choice to make: Ragnall can be fair for him by night, in which case she must be foul by day, or vice versa. After some hesitation Gawain asks Ragnall to choose, since she is just as much affected by the decision as he. Elated, Ragnall claps her hands and declares the spell entirely broken, saying that now she can be fair both by day and by night. As you may have guessed, the one true answer to Gromer's question is: What women most desire is the freedom to choose who they will be!

This extraordinary story shows us another dimension to the challenge theme. Here we see the challenge of summer, which parallels the challenge of winter offered by the Green Knight. But here the central character of the story is feminine. In Ragnall, we have one of the few literary appearances of the Green Woman. Her challenge is a very real one, both for Gawain and for those of us today who can hear the story's message. Aside from its theme of justice and freedom for women, a further aspect that relates directly to our investigation of the Green Man presents itself.

Ragnall can be seen as representing the angry face of nature, which we may easily experience as "ugly," in response to our abuse. But Ragnall, the Green

> Ragnall, the Green Woman, can teach us a great deal about our relationship to the environment, as the Green Man has always tried to do.

king offer the answer the old woman gave him. Gromer flies into a rage, because only one person, his sister Ragnall, could possibly have known the one true answer that could save Arthur's life!

Happy to have his head, but miserable for his nephew, Arthur returns to court with Ragnall and breaks the bad news to Gawain. Gawain, a model of courtesy as ever, agrees to the match, though women everywhere wail at the loss of the handsome hero to the dreadful hag.

The pair are married in high style and retire to the bridal chamber. When Ragnall requests a kiss, Gawain, summoning up his courage, complies. At once the loathly creature is transformed into a beautiful young woman! She explains that she and Gromer had been enchanted by Morgan le Fay;

ABOVE: Holly, green throughout the year, is the symbol of the Green Knight's enduring strength.

RIGHT: This spot, at Hoo Brook, Staffordshire, is traditionally considered the site of the Green Chapel.

Woman, can teach us a great deal about our relationship to the environment, as the Green Man has always tried to do. She tells us that, just as Ragnall wants to *choose* how she will express herself, so nature desires to be allowed to follow its own course, to grow how and where it will, unchecked by human beings. If we permit this to happen, we will receive the wisdom of the natural world.

However, if we ignore nature's messages, it will remain ugly to us, and show us only its cruel face.

THE GREEN MAN OF KNOWLEDGE

Sir Gawain and the Green Knight and *Bricriu's Feast* are not the only places in which the Green Gome proffers his challenge. A story that recurs throughout Celtic folk tradition, with close parallels in the folklore of

people as far-flung as the users of Esquimaux and Sanskrit, shows how the Green Man finds new ways to insinuate himself into our consciousness.

In the Celtic tradition this folktale is known as *The Green Man of Knowledge*. It recounts the adventures of "Jack" who, after a life of carefree idleness, decides to try his luck in the world and eventually finds his way into the Land of Enchantment. There he meets the Green Man of Knowledge and manages to defeat him at a game of cards. Then Jack follows the Green Man home and seeks the hand of his fair young daughter in marriage. He wins her by way of a series of seemingly impossible tasks, which he finally accomplishes only with the help of the daughter herself.

The fact that the same story, with some local variants, occurs in both Ireland, where it is called either *Green Leaf* or *Green Leverey*, and in Scotland, where it is known as *The Green Man of Knowledge* or *Green Sleeves*, shows how widespread it is and how deeply associated with the idea of the Green Man. There is even a Romany version, which was collected from a group of Welsh Gypsies, called *O Grino Murs Jivela are Kekeno T'em*, or "The Green Man who lived in Noman's Land."

MERRY ROBIN GOODFELLOW

The Green Man's challenge can be expressed in ways other than that of the Green Knight's game—namely, as trickery. We have seen that trickery is a prominent feature in the behavior of both the Green

The Fool is a representative of the Year Kings, who were given responsibility over the people for a brief time and then were sacrificed.

Knight and of Curoi. A third important figure who manifests this feature is a fairy being known as Robin Goodfellow. Almost everything we know about him comes from a curious seventeenth-century pamphlet that revels in the title *Robin Goodfellow, alias Puck, alias Hob: his mad pranks, and merry jests, full of honest mirth, and is a fit medicine for melancholy*. It was printed in 1628, but almost certainly drew on a whole range of existing fairy lore as well as elements drawn from the tales of Robin Hood and other Green Man traditions.

In this story, Oberon, the Fairy King, visits a maiden at night, but vanishes during the day "wither she knew not, he went so suddenly." The outcome of these nightly visits is a child, Robin Goodfellow, who shows no unusual traits until, at age six, he begins to play such tricks upon the neighbors that his mother despairs. She finally threatens to whip him, and since this "did not please him," he ran away. A day's journey from his home he went to sleep in a field and dreamed of bright-eyed folk who danced around him all night to music as beautiful as that which the Greek demigod Orpheus once coaxed from his lyre. In the morning Robin woke to find a scroll beside him on which was written in words of gold:

> *Robin, my only son and heir,*
> *How to live take thou no care:*
> *By nature thou hast cunning shifts,*
> *Which I'll increase with other gifts.*
> *Wish what thou wilt, thou shall it have;*
> *And for to fetch both fool and knave,*
> *Thou hast the power to change thy shape,*
> *To horse, to hog, to dog, to ape.*
> *Transformed thus, by any means,*
> *See none thou harm'st but knaves and queans:*
> *But love thou those that honest be,*
> *And help them in necessity.*
> *Do thus and all the world shall know*
> *The pranks of Robin Goodfellow,*
> *For by that name thou called shall be*
> *To age's last posterity;*
> *And if thou keep my just command,*
> *One day thou shall see Fairy Land.*

Robin first tested the promise of wish granting by asking for food, and a dish of fine veal was set before him. He wished for plum pudding: it appeared. Then, tired of eating, he wished to be a horse. Immediately he became a fine spirited beast. Then he changed himself into a black dog, a green tree, and so on, until he was sure he could change himself into anything he wanted. Then he decided to try out his newfound skills by playing more of the tricks for which his mother had threatened to beat him. So he set out into the world, where he pulled so many pranks that his name soon became known throughout the land. He played tricks on clowns, on burghers, and on old and young. Interestingly, he also turned himself into a chimney sweep. Finally, the complaints about his trickery were so great that his father Oberon summoned him to Fairy Land, where he is said to have remained for "many a long year."

ABOVE LEFT: A seventeenth-century woodcut shows Robin Goodfellow surrounded with a circle of witches or fairies.
ABOVE: Robin Hood, the medieval outlaw of Sherwood Forest, became an important figure in the mythology of the Green Man.

LEFT: *Robin Goodfellow in his most Puckish guise in this costume sketch for Shakespeare's* A Midsummer Night's Dream.
RIGHT: *The Fool supported by two dancing Wildmen, bringing together two aspects of the Green Man.*

THE LAUGHING SPRITE

In fact, Robin Goodfellow is a type of brownie, a hobgoblin or sprite, whose primary characteristics are both to cause trouble for mortals and to clean the houses of people who welcome such beings. This dual behavior is in keeping with the instructions Robin Goodfellow's father gives him in the scroll—namely, that he is to harm no one who does not deserve it. Indeed, the victims of his pranks are unworthy people. Even so, despite the anger he arouses by his at-times outrageous deeds, these deeds are not really spiteful or cruel. Like his namesake Robin Hood, he helps the poor at the expense of the rich.

Several other mythical characters share Robin Goodfellow's attributes of shape-shifting and trickiness. In Welsh myth, for example, we have Taliesin, a poet and shaman of the sixth century who, after drinking a magic brew from the cauldron of the goddess Ceridwen, acquires both wisdom and the capacity to shape shift. The same tradition also gives us the famous character of Merlin, who could change his shape at will, and who, on more than one occasion, played tricks on his adversaries, leaving the scenes of his antics with the deep chuckle that became his signature.

The association of Robin Goodfellow with such figures shows that he is more than a simple fairy. Like Robin Hood, he is a hero of the common people. And, like Merlin, he plays tricks that resolve mysteries and display his abilities to manifest supernatural effects. His characteristic "ho, ho, ho" is reminiscent of Merlin's laughter, while his shape-shifting abilities are like those of the Taliesin.

FOOL FOR A DAY

Stories of the Trickster lead us to a related figure—the Fool. As Lord of Misrule, the man chosen to play the Fool presided over the May Day games along with the Robin Hood and Green Jack impersonators. Crowned for a day, he was shown every courtesy, even though he represented a clownish chaos that most people feared during the rest of the year. As with so

many aspects of the archetype of the Green Man, the Fool represented an outlawed wildness we will encounter again in the next chapter.

The Puritan writer Phillip Stubbs paints a vivid, if somewhat disapproving, picture of the appointment and actions of the Fool:

> *First, all the wild-heads of the parish, coventing together, choose them a Grand-Captain (of all Mischief) whom they ennoble with the title "My Lord of Misrule," and him they crown with great solemnity, and adopt for their King.*

Having selected between twenty and a hundred men to accompany him, all of whom are dressed in costumes of green and gold, the Lord and his company proceed . . .

> *towards the church and churchyard, their pipes piping, their drummers thundering, their stumps dancing, their bells jingling, their handkerchiefs swinging about their heads like madmen, their hobby horses and other monsters skirmishing amongst the rout.*

Somewhat surprisingly, this noisy, brightly dressed group enters the church, whether or not a service is in progress, and dances before the altar. Then they go out again into the churchyard where, Stubbs says,

> *they have commonly their Summer Halls, their bowers, arbours and banqueting houses set up, wherein they feast, banquet and dance all that day and peradventure all the night too.*

The Fool and his men are then given food by the parishioners, to whom they sell "badges" which they called "My Lord of Misrule's Badges," and which protect their owners from the merciless mockery of the Lord's men.

As with the May Day revels, the antics of the Fool acted as a safety valve for the ordinary people, offering them a safe means of challenging the nobility who oppressed them so cruelly during the rest of the year. At another remove, the Fool is a representative of the Year Kings, who were given responsibility over the people for a brief time and then were sacrificed to insure the continued fertility of the land.

Trickster gods the world over are seen as playing a part in the creation of humanity.

We would not be wrong in seeing Robin Goodfellow as a type of Fool and a native British trickster akin to the Native American Coyote, or the West Indian Anansi, both of whom possess qualities of clownish defiance.

Trickster gods the world over are seen as playing a part in the creation of humanity. After this creation they maintain an unpredictable relationship with their "offspring," a connection that often manifests in the form of tricks and games apparently intended to keep us on our emotional, intellectual, and spiritual toes!

This quality of sly trickery is also apparent in the foliate heads with their impish, mocking faces. Others who display these tricksterish characteristics of the Green Man include the Wild Man, the Wild Herdsman, and Herne the Hunter, figures that we will encounter in the next chapter.

RIGHT: The chalk hill figure of a giant from Cerne Abbas in Dorset, England, represents the ancient earthy power of the primitive Green Man.

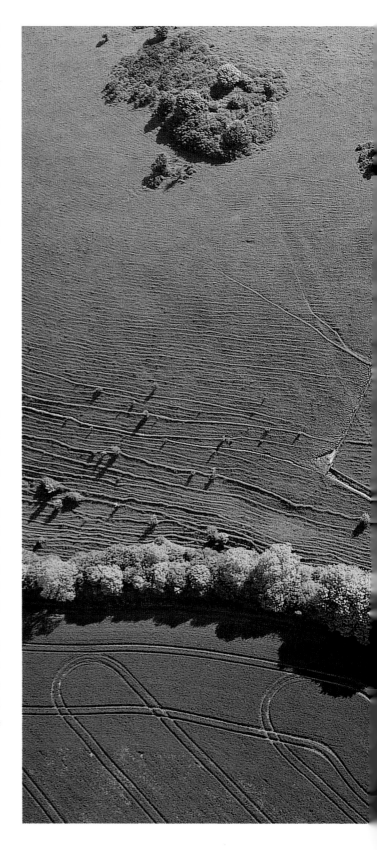

MEDITATION

THE GREEN GIANT

Close your eyes and prepare to set out on a journey. As your familiar surroundings fade, you find yourself in a sunlit glade deep within the wildwood. It is evening, and the sun sends golden shafts of light between the sentinel trees. You stretch your length on the inviting turf and, as you listen to the drowsy hum of bees, you fall deeply asleep and begin to dream.

You are standing by a low green mound in the side of which gapes a dark hole. A cold wind blows from it, and you shiver. Then a rustling sound announces the appearance of an awesome figure. Standing over eight feet high, he is clad in leaves. Leaves sprout from his mouth, his nostrils, from the corners of his eyes. His arms and legs are like branches and his fingers and toes like twigs. His movements sound like wind blowing through a grove of trees.

For a moment you are afraid; for such raw power is emitted by this being that you can scarcely stand before it. Then you become aware of a deep assurance, a feeling of abiding friendship, conveyed to you without word or sign from the mighty figure.

Now the powerful being gestures for you to follow him. You do so, running to keep up with his great strides. At last you come to a sheltered hollow between massive rocks. Great trees bend round the rocks and overhang the cave-like hollow. In front of the cave stands a worn block of stone, and leaning against the stone is a huge stone ax. The leaf-man turns toward you, and once again a message is conveyed, though no words are uttered.

You fall back in horror as you realize what the tree-man is asking you to do—take up the ax and cut off his head! Again there is a reassurance—that all will be well if you do as he wishes.

Slowly the Green Man kneels, his mighty knees cracking like breaking branches. Hesitating, you pick up the ax, surprised by its lightness. With growing confidence and a wave of subtle energy, you heft the ax, raise it high above the bending figure,

bring it down, and cut through the neck of the Green Man.

You jump back, expecting a rush of blood, but only a few drops that seem more like sap than blood emerge from the headless neck. The tree-like figure remains bent over the stone, as if becoming rooted to the spot, but the head has disappeared!

Then, where the drops of blood sap had fallen, you see a stirring in the earth, and green shoots appear from the ground. You watch in astonishment as one grows rapidly to become a tall ear of corn, while another becomes a young sapling, covered in tender green leaves.

As you continue to look, a face appears amid the leaves of the sapling. It is a laughing face with wide lips from which leaves are starting to sprout. It is the face of the Green Man!

before—except that a new tree is growing beside the ancient stone, and the ax is once again in place beside it.

At the entrance to the mound the Green Man turns toward you, and this time you hear words forming in your mind: "You have witnessed the

Now he grows with astonishing rapidity, until he is taller than you, his face resembling more and more the tree-man you killed. Suddenly, he pulls both of his feet from the earth and sets off for the green mound. You follow him, glancing back at the clearing, where all now seems just as it was

death and rebirth of the year. Wherever you walk in the world you will now see and hear and feel the voices of growing things. Go now, and take this, my gift of nature-wisdom."

The Green Man extends a large, twig-like hand to you. A hazel nut lies on the rough palm. You take the nut, and eat it, understanding that it is a seed of wisdom that will take root and grow within you.

Now you turn from this magical scene and return to the place where you began to dream. You slip back into your body and begin to wake up. Return now to your normal consciousness, but remember all that you have experienced in the place in your soul where the Green Man dwells eternally.

Chapter Six

The Wildman and the Wodewose

There are mushrooms for a brain,
owl talons, vervain, mandrake,
and something else, unnamed,
that sets the shallow winter sap upon its face
and grants the Greenman motion
and binds him to the forest waste.

Ari Berk, *Anatomies*

Wildness is everywhere, in the growth of nature and in the stirring of the human heart when we are moved to anger, love, or fear. The archetype of the Wildman from the ancient and medieval worlds is an expression of the soul's freedom to choose, to make its own way in the world. It also expresses a natural inclination toward a wildness of spirit that we ignore at our peril—physical, psychological, and spiritual. By acknowledging the Wildman we can learn a great deal about our own relationships, not only to each other, but also to the natural world. The face he presents expresses the Green Man's anger at the way we have failed to maintain our unwritten contract with nature—our own and that of the planet.

THE FACE OF WILDNESS

As we have seen, many of the representations of the Green Man act as either adversaries or challengers. In the Middle Ages the Wildman became a personification of those aspects of nature—vegetative, animal, and human—rejected by humankind in its espousal of civilization. By challenging the very premises of civilization, the Wildman became the object of many of the most deep-seated fears of the medieval Christian world, exemplified in particular by the reaction of the established Church to the ungovernable or unlicensed behavior represented by the traditional May Day celebrations.

For this reason the medieval Wildman was thought of as living in remote corners of the land, especially forests, mountains, and caves. He is described as:

a hairy man curiously compounded of human and animal traits, without, however, sinking to the level of an ape. It exhibits upon its naked human anatomy a growth of fur, leaving bare only its face, feet, and hands, at times its knees and elbows, or the breasts of the female of the species. Frequently the creature is shown wielding a heavy club or mace, or the trunk of a tree.

(Bernheimer, *Wild Men In the Middle Ages*)

ABOVE: The Wildman leads the way into the heart of the forest.

RIGHT: This ancient tree stump epitomizes the sometimes fearsome energy of the Wildman's natural home.

Though often represented as clothed in long hair, which can be alternately matted and filthy or carefully groomed, there are also descriptions in which the Wildman is covered in a growth of leaves, which seem to be part of him rather than an artificially constructed covering. Even in his hairiest form he generally wears a circlet of leaves, or has leaves draped around his loins. Clearly, he is yet one more aspect of the Green Man.

THE FIRST WILDMEN

The earliest accounts we have of human representatives of the Wildman come from classical and preclassical times; they range from such characters as Enkidu in the Sumerian *Epic of Gilgamesh*, whom we met in chapter 1, to the Greek poet Orpheus, who shared many of the attributes of the dying and rising gods after he journeyed to the Underworld to reclaim his wife Euridice. Orpheus's connection with the spirit of wildness comes through his close association with the nature god Dionysus who, as we also saw in chapter 1,

ABOVE: An early-sixteenth-century foliate head decorates a bench in Bishop's Lydeard Church, Somerset, England.

represented an ungovernable wildness of spirit for much of the classical world.

A typical story expressing the terrifying power of Dionysus tells how the three daughters of King Minyas were reluctant to honor the god and scolded the other women of the court for going off into the mountains to celebrate his orgiastic mysteries. Learning of their disdain, Dionysus confronted the errant women, appearing first as a bull, then a lion,

> This story, terrible though it is, warns those who would deny the wildness that is part of our own nature, as well as of the earth.

and finally as a leopard. With his coming, ivy and vines grew over the chair where Minyas's daughters did their weaving, and serpents crawled in their baskets of wool. Terrified, the women promised to sacrifice one of their children to the god, and having drawn lots they tore the unfortunate infant to pieces. Banished for this terrible crime, they wandered the hills until they were metamorphosed by Dionysus into the shapes of a bat, an owl, and a crow.

This story, terrible though it is, warns those who would deny the wildness that is part of our own nature, as well as of the earth. Such denial invites that same force to invade our world. If you shut out your wildness, it will come to get you.

VISIONS IN THE WILD

There is something inherently disturbing in these images of the Wildman who simultaneously displays both human and nonhuman qualities. Our species tends to marginalize what it fears, and during the Middle Ages and earlier the Wildman was treated as an object of fear. At the heart of this treatment of the archetype lies a tension between two distinct portraits of the Wildman—on the one hand, as a

ABOVE: The face of Merlin looks out from this carving in the living
rock of Alderley Edge, Cheshire, England.

potentially friendly being, and, on the other, as a savage
creature. This echoes the most common perception of
the Green Man, allowing him to be portrayed as at
once kind and helpful and fearsome and aggressive.

This dichotomy arose in part from the way nature
itself was perceived; that is, as both kindly and
threatening—more often the latter. This perception
of threat can be seen in the medieval stories about
people who went mad and became wildmen as the
result of witnessing violent events. Interestingly, the
Wildman's madness conveyed wisdom as well as
wildness on those who succumbed to it.

A powerful example of this wise madness can be
seen in the character of Merlin, the shaman, seer, and
prophet who ran mad in the forest after witnessing

the carnage of the battle of Arderrydd. Actually, Merlin had already exhibited a number of Wildman characteristics before this event. The offspring of a royal princess and a demon, or fairy, he was born hairy as a sign of this "demonic" origin. However, his hairy pelt fell from him when he was baptized; this signified that the pagan wildness within him had been tamed by the civilizing influence of Christianity.

It was later, as a fully grown man, that Merlin underwent his period of madness, which paradoxically put him in touch with his original wildness in such a way that he could fully utilize its power to become a visionary. During his time of madness in the woods, with only a tame pig to talk to, the gift of prophecy came to him, so that he was able to utter curious verses to his companion:

> *Listen little pig.*
> *Wonders there will be*
> *In Prydein—but I*
> *Shall not care.*
> *When the people of Mona*
> *Ask questions of the Brython,*
> *That will be a troublesome time!*
> *A superior lord will appear:*
> *Cynan, from the banks of the Teiwi*
> *Confusion will follow—*
> *But we shall have the music of the Bards!*
> (John Matthews, trans.)

THE WILD HERDSMAN

Because of their death to normal consciousness and their rebirth into extraordinary consciousness, or wisdom, through madness, the embodiments of the Wildman aspect of the Green Man were regarded as repositories of earthy knowledge. Hence Merlin was one of the Wildman's avatars. People sought out these dwellers in the wilderness in order to gain their wisdom, including their knowledge of herbs and plants for healing and of simples and potions for problems ranging from sprained muscles to unrequited love.

The Wildman's deep understanding and love and knowledge of nature also made him a sought-after herdsman, able to gather animals to him and to converse with them. In this form, as the Lord of the Animals, he appears in a number of medieval stories.

We find one of the most detailed of such portraits in the twelfth-century French Arthurian romance of *Yvain*, written by the well-known court poet Chretien de Troyes. In the story, the hero, lost in the legendary Forest of Broceliande, encounters a herd of wild bulls who repeatedly charge each other with great savagery, filling the woods with the din of their battle. Watching over this strange scene is an even stranger figure:

> *. . . his head was bigger than that of a horse or any other beast . . . his hair was in tufts, leaving his forehead bare for a width of more than two spans . . . his ears were big and mossy, just like those of an elephant; his eyebrows were heavy and his face was flat; his eyes were those of an owl, and his nose was like a cat's; his jowls were split like a wolf, and his teeth were sharp and yellow like a wild boar's; his beard was black and his whiskers twisted; his chin merged into his chest and his backbone was long, but twisted and hunched. There he stood, leaning upon his club and accoutred in a strange garb, consisting not of cotton or wool, but rather the hides recently flayed from two bulls.* (W. W. Comfort, trans.)

In the Celtic counterpart of Chretien's story: *Owein, or the Knight of the Ravens*, the otherworldly aspect of the character is even more noticeable. Here the herdsman is more specifically described as a guardian of the animals and is first glimpsed surrounded by wild creatures, sitting on top of a mound. Taller than two normal men, he has a single eye and one foot. When asked a question, he strikes a huge stag with his club so that it bellows, summoning more animals who then gather about their lord like courtiers.

Taken together, these references point to a connection with shamanism, that ancient spiritual discipline still found in cultures the world over, whose practitioners were, as they continue to be today, closely connected with the energies of nature—both vegetative and animal. The primary function of these guardians of wisdom is to journey out of the body, to visit the Otherworld, and to return from such journeys with information for the communities they serve. It is believed that they can shape-shift, most often into the form of animal, bird, or fish. In effect, they give voice to the hidden world of the spirit, making them perfect mediators of the Green Man.

RETURN TO THE WILD

The banishment of the Wildman may account for the fact that he is often said to live only in those places deemed unfit for human habitation—wilderness and wild, untamed tracts such as Edmund Spencer romanticizes in *The Faerie Queene*:

LEFT: This dancing Siberian shaman exhibits many attributes of the Green Man.

BELOW: The fearsome figure of the wild herdsman from Celtic myth exhibits aspects of the Green Man in his guise as guardian of the animals. From a painting by Roger Garland.

Far in the forest by a hollow glade,
Covered with massy shrubs, which spreading broads
Did underneath them make a gloomy shade;
Where foot of living creature neverr trod
Nor scarce wild beast dare come, there was this
wight's abode
(Bk 6, canticle 4, stanza xi)

Wildman lore suggests that he is so much a part of nature that he can only dwell in such wild spots and avoids those places tamed by humankind, retreating ever deeper into the wilderness to escape the excesses of civilization—its cruelty, greed, and hypocrisy. This idea is conveyed by a German poem composed around 1545, where the Wildman himself addresses us:

We find the things of evil sort
Embraced by all society
While all the best variety
Is driven out or just destroyed
A man who would be well employed
And finds the world in such a mess
Must forsake this faithlessness
And so we left our worldly goods
To make our home in these deep woods
With our little ones protected
From the falsehood we rejected
We feed ourselves on native fruits
And from the earth dig tender roots
For drink pure springs are plentiful
For warmth sunlight is bountiful
For garment grass and leaves we take
And from the same our beds we make
Our homes are made in caves of stone
And no one takes what's not his own
The wild beasts which most men fear
We find are good companions here.
(Fred A. Childs, trans., *Lament of the Wildfolk Over*
the Perfidious World)

The ambiguity of our experience of nature expressed in this poem lies at the heart of the Wildman's story and accounts for the contradictions in the way he is described. Like nature itself, the Wildman can by turns be violent and aggressive, gentle and kindly.

THE WILD WOMAN

For medieval people, the Wildman did not live in total isolation. Wild Women are, if anything, more numerous than Wildmen. They appear frequently as gentle spirits of trees and woodland, dressed in leaves, their flowing hair contrasting with their wizened faces. In some areas of Europe they were believed to grow to a huge size, and so to resemble giantesses and ogres. Elsewhere, they were known as "Blessed Damsels" and recognized as offering wisdom and kindness to those who sought them out. We know very little about the Green Woman as such, and certainly there are few female faces among the foliate heads, but many of the aspects of the Green Man are partnered by a female aspect who bears identical or similar attributes to those we have come recognize in him. Thus Lady Bercilak shadows the Green Knight, Marian stands beside the figure of Robin Hood, Isis mirrors Osiris, and the Wildman of the Middle Ages often has both "wife" and "children" companioning him in his exile.

ABOVE: *Rare images of Green Women from two Roman capitals.*
They are surrounded by fruit and vines as an expression of their
abundant natural energy.
RIGHT: *In this medieval illustration the Wildman joins the fools*
and dancers of the European folk tradition.

AN ONGOING TRADITION

During the Renaissance and afterward, in the seventeenth and eighteenth centuries, the concept of the Wildman became synonymous with the romantic, though essentially unrealistic, idea of the "noble savage." For example, philosophers like Rousseau advocated a "back to nature" mode of simplified living. For a while this ideal was enormously popular, but in time it was replaced by the values of modern society, which has placed more and more importance on possessions and control over the environment, rather than on partnership with it.

The response of the Wildman to civilization shows itself in stories that depict him as sitting huddled under a rain cloud while the rest of the land basks in sunlight. Then, when the clouds roll in and rain descends, the Wildman laughs and dances! Such uncivilized behavior shows that he possesses the same trickster energy we have met before in the Green Man's various representatives. In each case, their

determination to behave in a contrary way is an inherent part of their untamed natures. Part of the repertoir of the folk players at whom we will look more closely in the next chapter was to behave foolishly and to caper and prance and play tricks on

Wild Women appear frequently as gentle spirits of trees and woodland, dressed in leaves, their flowing hair contrasting with their wizened faces.

those who watched. This is a very ancient idea, dating back as far as we can see. Shamans have always acted in a wild, strange, and clownish manner. This behavior is echoed as well in the uninhibited customs of the May Day revels, and in the madness of the Fool's court when, as we have seen, the laws of the workaday world were turned upside down and the patterns of daily drudgery were interrupted in the name of delight.

THE WILDNESS OF NATURE

As previously suggested, the Wildman is wild in part because he expresses an aspect of the Green Man that is angry. It is as though, as humankind imposed an ever increasing degree of control and destructiveness over the environment, the Green Man sent these alarming emissaries to inform us that he was less than pleased with what we were doing! It is as

though, as humanity continued to distance itself from the natural world, it saw wildness in a less and less positive way. What had once been perceived as a friendly environment, shared with animals and utilized for food, clothing, medicine, and shelter, gradually transformed itself into something to be feared and dominated.

During the Middle Ages the notion that humanity had a divine right to subdue nature was pursued to excess. This destructive—ultimately self-destructive —idea led directly to the environmental nightmare that surrounds us today. Strip-mining and the wholesale deforestation of millions of square miles of rain forest, decimated to fill the pockets of greedy developers, is only a part of the story. Farmland has been systematically overused until it is virtually

> In the madness of the fool's court, laws of the workaday world were turned upside down and the patterns of daily drudgery were interrupted in the name of delight.

barren, and now, in recent times, we have even begun to manipulate the genetic structure of the green world to grow "improved" crops, vegetables, and fruit.

No wonder the aspect of the Green Man that first came to the fore in the Middle Ages was the Wildman! No wonder he is still angry! It is time we looked again at what we have already done, and at what we are still doing, to the earth! Only in this way may we assuage the Wildman's anger and relate to him in a healthy, natural way.

LEFT: The gnarled and hairy body of the Wildman emphasizes his difference from the rest of humanity.
RIGHT: A portrait of the Green Man by artist Felicity Bowers perhaps portrays his anger at our treatment of the environment.

THE GREEN HUNTSMAN

A character who forms an important link between the vegetative, animal, and human aspects of the Green Man is Herne the Hunter. Over the centuries he has assumed the mantle of earlier archetypes, including that of the Norse god Woden, a leader of the Wild Hunt.

The first known recorded mention of Herne is in 1623, in Shakespeare's *The Merry Wives of Windsor*. In act IV, scene 4, Mistress Page recounts the following legend:

> *There is an old tale goes, that Herne the hunter,*
> *Sometime a keeper here in Windsor forest,*
> *Doth all the winter-time, at still midnight,*
> *Walk round about an oak, with great ragg'd horns—*
> *And there he blasts the tree, and takes the cattle,*
> *And makes the milch-kine yield blood, and shakes a chain*
> *In a most hideous and dreadful manner. . . .*
> *You have heard of such a spirit, and well you know*
> *The superstitious idle-headed eld*
> *Received, and did deliver to our age,*
> *This tale of Herne the hunter for a truth.*

Despite the doubt about the archetypal reality of Herne and his effect on earlier people expressed in these last lines, there is clear indication that the story is an old one. We know Shakespeare's knowledge of folklore was considerable and that he seldom invents when he can refer to a genuine story. A variant

ABOVE: The horned god of the Celts represents the oldest image of the green huntsman.

version of the above scene, altered by an anonymous author who probably lived in the Windsor area, adds the following:

Oft have you heard since Horne the hunter [sic] dyed
That women to affright their little children,
Ses that he walkes in shape of a great stagge.
Now for that Falstaffe hath been so deceived,
As that he dare not venture to the house,
Weele send him word to meet vs in the field,
Disguised like Horne, with huge horns on his head,
The houre shal be iust betweene twelue and one,
And at that time we will meet him both:
Then would I have you present there at hand,
With little boyes disguided and dressed like Fayries,
For to affright fat Falstaffe in the woods.

Here Herne is clearly associated with the fairy race and is depicted as wearing horns, a fact that helps us identify him as something more than a simple "keeper here in Windsor forest." Whatever story Shakespeare knew, it seems likely that the author of these additional lines knew better. He seems to have drawn upon an older story associated with Windsor Great Park which, until the seventeenth century, proudly displayed "Herne's Oak," an enormous, ancient tree supposedly the site of visitations by a mysterious and terrifying huntsman and his ghostly hounds.

References to Herne as leader of the Wild Hunt are found in many cultures throughout the ages. A dramatic nineteenth-century account from Sweden gives us an idea of their effect on the locals:

Sometimes, if you sleep with an open window during the summer, when the weather is fine and the nights are light, you might suddenly be woken up by a frightful hurly-burly out in the forest, right behind the house. There is shrieking and shouting, and the barking of a whole pack of dogs, the thud of horse hoofs, the cracking of broken branches and so on. It's dreadful, and it's no time to be out in the forest, for the hind hunt's on. You shake and quiver and
your heart pounds at the sound of it. Sleeping's out of the question. If you're brave enough to take a peep out of the window in spite of it—O good gracious, seeing the hind hunt is even worse than hearing it!

Other accounts verify the fear experienced by all who merely hear, let alone see, the Hunt. Its coming is often announced by a terrible din, flashes of

ABOVE: *Herne the Hunter haunts Windsor Great Park to this day.*
A nineteenth-century engraving by George Cruikshank.

lightening, wind in the tree tops, the rattling of chains, and the ringing of bells—scenes reminiscent of the Green Knight's entrance into King Arthur's court. The Hunter is described as carrying a whip, wearing antlers, and having a skull for a face—or no face at all! In Germany, it is said that an old man named Honest Eckart goes in front of the Hunt, warning people to get out of the way. Eckart is often described, like Woden or Odin, as having a long grey beard and a broad-brimmed hat, and as riding a white horse. In one version of the story he calls out:

Fly then, quickly, make no stay
For Herne the Hunter rides this way.

In the Welsh story "Pwyll Prince of Dyfed," the prince encounters the underworld king Arawn with his ghostly pack.

> *And of all the hounds he had seen in the world, he had seen no dogs the colour of these. The colour that was on them was a brilliant shining white, and their ears red; and as the whiteness of their bodies shone, so did the redness of their ears glisten. . . . And . . . he saw a horseman coming towards him upon a large light-grey steed, with a hunting horn round his neck, and clad in garments of grey.*

This image of the Huntsman is augmented by accounts of Gwynn ap Nudd, who dwells beneath Glastonbury Tor and leads his pack of hounds to hunt in the cultivated lands on certain feast days. Gwynn, as we saw in chapter 2, is one of the figures who abducts the Flower Bride and who fights for the Spring Maiden every Midsummer Eve.

So the Huntsman is horned, rides a wild horse, and leads a pack of hounds—or sometimes wild men—over the hills. In most accounts, he chases the souls of the dead, capturing them and carrying them off to the Otherworld. These are all characteristics that help us identify the Huntsman. Herne springs from the Saxon tradition, and it is to this cultural milieu that we must look for his origins.

WODEN AND THE HOODENERS

Woden (or Odin) is the premier god of the Norse people. He is a father-god, like the Greek Zeus, the Roman Jupiter, or the Irish Dagda. He brings life and fertility to his people, as well as the wisdom of the runes, which he discovers by sacrificing himself to himself for nine nights on a windy tree. He is also a god of the hunt, and trees are sacred to him. These are all aspects we can recognize as belonging to the Green Man in his several guises.

Etymologically, the names Woden and Herne are connected. When Woden leads his select band of warriors, the *herjar*, he is given the name Herian, which mutates into Harilo, Hevela, Herlake, Herla—and, later on, Herne. The Herlingas, referred to by the Anglo-Saxon poet Widsith, are the followers of Woden's *herjar*. Norse tradition tells us further that Woden rides an eight-legged horse named Sleipnir, reminiscent of the Oss in English folk dances. Herne

ABOVE: The Celtic Gundrestrup Cauldron shows a wild-faced god surrounded by men and animals over whom he has absolute power.
RIGHT: This Roman horned head from St. Albans is a precursor of later characters from the mythology of the Green Man.

also rides a wild horse sometimes said to have two legs, sometimes six or eight.

Herne was associated with the cult of the dead, as was the stag whose antlers he wears. The combination of this terrible horse with its spectral rider suggests a long history of interconnected traditions dealing with a phantom hunter who chases the souls of the dead, leads a pack of white hounds, and rides through the heavens.

TO WEAR THE HORNS

The whole subject of "wearing the horns" is actually of considerable interest. Despite the Christian identification of horned beings with the devil (called "Old Horney" in some parts of England because of his permanent state of arousal), throughout much of Europe horned beings were benignly remembered by the common people as embodiments of potency and fertility.

Herne the Hunter is directly linked to Robin Goodfellow by an illustration that accompanied some of the earlier editions of his *Merry Pranks* in which he is depicted as leading a group of dancers. Here Robin is horned, wears a hunting horn slung round his neck, and carries a distinctly phallic staff. Similarly, an entry in the *Chronicle of Lanercost Priory* for 1282 mentions a religious lapse of a certain parish priest, who during Easter week gathered a party of girls from local villages and led them in a circle dance, while he carried a pole displaying "the human organs of reproduction"!

Traditions still extant that reflect the importance of wearing or carrying horns include the famous Abbots Bromley Horn Dance, performed by a team of dancers every September at the village of Abbots Bromley in Staffordshire. In the dance six men carry sets of very old antlers, accompanied by a man dressed as Maid Marian, a Fool with a bladder, and a boy with a bow and arrows. This latter figure is identified with Robin Hood. The dance may well be the last remnant of a far older ceremony, perhaps as old as prehistoric times, in which a shaman performed rituals enacting and celebrating successful deer hunts.

Shakespeare, who as we know was familiar with many of the ancient traditions of England, preserves another old song in *As You Like It*. Here the clown Jaques sings:

> *What shall he have that killed the deer?*
> *His leather skin and horns to wear.*
> *Then sing him home:*
> *Take no scorn to wear the horn;*
> *It was a crest ere thou wast born.*
> *They father's father wore it;*
> *And they father bore it.*
> *The horn, the horn, the lusty horn,*
> *Is not a thing to laugh to scorn.*

These lines convey the idea that the wearing of the horns was once a confirmation of lustiness as well as being a reward for having slain the deer, itself a symbol of nature's fecundity.

ABOVE LEFT: The face of the Green Man with the horns of the Huntsman and Lord of the Animals is depicted in this stained glass window from a church in Pennel, Wales.
RIGHT: These dancing Wildmen have been invited to perform before the civilized medieval court.

WILDMEN DANCING

The Green Man and the Wildman are closely related aspects of the same archetype in their strength, ferocity, and green otherworldliness. Both, too, are connected with trees. In some instances the Wildman's very life essence is bound up with a particular tree, so that when it is in danger of being damaged or cut down he angrily appears to defend it. This becomes a powerful ecological statement if applied to the wanton destruction of so much of the world's forests in our own time. We can see why both the Green Man and the Wildman have come to epitomize certain aspects of the Green Movement.

The Green Man's presence reminds us that wildness can be a liberating force in our daily lives and that wholesale environmental destruction is likely to lead to our own demise. At the hearts of many people today is an aching hollow of sadness; those who are able to articulate it often express a feeling of grief at the loss of their immediate contact with the natural world. Instead of acknowledging our partnership with the ecosystem, we have sought to either possess it or separate ourselves from it, resulting in our increasing isolation from each other. We have made stone prisons for ourselves, locked the doors, and thrown away the keys.

The Green Man's archetypal presence reminds us of other possibilities. By honoring the natural energy he personifies, we may yet find a way to reintegrate ourselves into our natural environment. If we succeed, we will certainly find the Green Man waiting for us, holding out the hand of fellowship, as we envision the possibility of a new earthly paradise, or at least of rediscovering the lost greenness of our own souls.

ABOVE: The Wildman *by Paul Klee perhaps signifies the fragmented nature he personifies.*

ABOVE RIGHT: An atmospheric view toward the site of Merlin's grave at Drumelzier, England.

AND STILL I AM THE GREEN MAN

Under the green woods
I walk alone.
Once all the fields were mine.
And the trees were mine.
The hills,
The spired coppices,
The straight drills.

Now I must share them—
With tractor-stink,
with harvest-slasher—
But I still find ways
To slip the seeds back
Into the furrow,
To watch them grow—
Remembered,
or forgot.

And still I am the Green Man
And still I walk the fields,
And though the Land seems empty
It is filled with life,
And though I am forgotten
I still remember,
And I still observe.

John Matthews

MEDITATION

A VISION OF HERNE

Close your eyes and prepare to set out on a journey. As your everyday consciousness fades, another scene opens up to you. It is of a woodland glade in sunlight. Birds sing overhead, and you hear the scutter of small feet in the undergrowth beneath the trees. It is a peaceful, quiet place, far from the noise and demands of your outer life. Indeed, so peaceful do you feel that when you see a moss-grown bank beneath the shade of a mighty oak tree, you throw yourself down and fall immediately into a deep sleep. And as you sleep, you begin to dream. . . .

In your dream you are in a different place, under bright stars at midnight. You find yourself walking along a great avenue of trees that leads to a natural amphitheater carved out of a hillside. On all sides are tall, unfamiliar trees. The moon is full overhead and casts a pale light over the scene. You see a figure moving and pause to watch.

Suddenly you begin to hear strange unearthly music, unlike anything you have known before. You see a tall figure dressed in a green cloak, moving to and fro in time to the music. The hood of the cloak is pulled up so that you can see neither face nor form. But you are awed by the figure's height; you feel great energy radiating from him.

As the figure moves, you see that it is tracing a complex pattern of silvery lines on the earth. Try as you will, you cannot grasp the meaning of the pattern. You watch in fascination as the figure completes a slow circling dance and then leaves.

Next come a group of forest sprites, dressed in the colors of the woodland—green and grey and brown, orange and russet and purple—shades that blur before your eyes as the sprites dance and circle in front of you.

Now more figures come—tall and imposing, in robes of shifting colors that seem to change from one moment to the next. Light radiates from the robes, as though they were transparencies draped over silver and gold flames. Others attend them— beings who seem part animal, part human, who move with such grace they can be of no mortal race.

Together, the whole group of entities joins in a dance that seems somehow to reflect the unearthly music and the pattern drawn by the hooded being. Now your own feet begin to twitch, and you can no longer sit still. You leap up and join the dancers, who make way for you and allow you to become part of the pattern they weave with their dance. Though you do not know either music or the dance steps, your feet are somehow caught up in the pattern, and you move as surely as any of the rest.

How long you dance you cannot say, but gradually the rhythm slows until everyone is spiraling slowly inward toward a natural throne set in the midst of tumbled rocks, where wild flowers cluster in rich and brilliant array. You focus on the tall figure, but now the green cloak is thrown open and the hood is pushed back from the great head.

Unforgettably, the figure rises before you, standing on human legs, but raising a head crowned with antlers like those of a great stag. You seem to see stars caught among the branching tines, and in the eyes that gaze down upon you are reflections of numberless dreams. You see your own hopes reflected there, as well as those of all humanity— too many and too great to understand. The eyes of Herne look into and beyond you, and you hear, in the depths of your spirit, a message for you alone.

For a timeless moment, you remain part of the fairy folk, standing before Herne the Hunter in the place of midnight. Then Herne bows his antlered head, and the dancers again move to a glorious paean of music that lifts them, and you, into the air above the trees and scatters you all like leaves.

The dancers circle the throne like stars, and you perceive for a moment their true light. Then you are floating, floating on a gentle breath toward the ground, where you see yourself, still sleeping beneath the great oak.

Coming to rest, you slowly awaken, and as you slip into everyday consciousness, you find you have come home to the place from where you began. The words of Herne the Hunter are still in your head, and as you wake you write down his message.

Chapter Seven

The Greening of the Soul

His tongue a leaf from the flower bowl
his mouth lips moulded from a wheel
his arms from wreath of apple boughs
holds in his gentle hand an apple . . .

Eric Mottram, *Green Man*

The green energy which spreads though everything that lives and moves upon this earth is present in us today—if we choose to acknowledge it. When we destroy the environment, we kill something of this energy in ourselves as well as in the planet. By preserving it we open more deeply to an awareness of life that can restore us with a new sense of vitality and well-being.

VERIDITAS

As we have seen, the Green Man, as the spirit of greenness, appears in literature, art, and popular imagination. He is also present in the folk plays which, from the Middle Ages onward, became an expression of human longing for the greening of life. The great twelfth-century mystic, Hildegard of Bingen, called this longing *viriditas*, the "greenness" of the soul, and so demonstrates that even within Christianity, the spirit of nature was present. The people of the Middle Ages saw "dryness" of soul as aridity and celebrated the "moisture" of the soul as

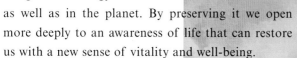

ABOVE: Holly, the symbol of nature's evergreen renewal. Here artist Andy Goldsworthy captures its secret elemental quality.
RIGHT: Druids burned huge fires of pine and yew at the Winter Solstice to draw back the sun god from the Underworld.

the juice or sap of life. Nowhere is this more evident than in medieval dance, which maintained the verdant glory of the spirit attuned to the body. But though the clerics saw dancing as lascivious, they did not hesitate to use it in their own sacred dramas.

THE MUMMERS AND THEIR PLAYS

Pre-Christian dances such as the Morris dance found yet another outlet in folk plays still performed throughout Europe today by groups of men called "mummers." The word may derive from the Danish word *mumme*, meaning "to disguise oneself with a mask." Another name for the players is "guisers," as in "dis-guise," reflecting the common theme of a human actor hiding behind the appearance of another—often sacred—being.

Mummers plays probably grew out of the rituals of ancient male societies in which the guardians of the Mysteries performed secret dramas. This probability has led one commentator to describe these plays as one of the most widespread examples of men's rituals to survive into this century.

Originally, either consciously or unconsciously, the Church itself copied the plays in its own promotion of sacred dramas based on biblical themes. Then the

two forms coexisted: side by side with the liturgical dramas, a large number of the older secular plays continued to be presented every year at seasonal high points such as Midwinter and Midsummer. All were performed by ordinary people, and fierce rivalries existed between towns as to which had the oldest and most authentic version—of which there were many.

Importantly, in the many hundreds of versions collected in Britain alone, virtually every one of the plays features a character who is killed and brought back to life. Often the death is by beheading, recalling the ancient motif of the dying and rising god we have seen in such stories as *Sir Gawain and the Green Knight* and such customs as the Garland Day celebrations.

ABOVE: This wooden figure by Lyle Skinner shows how the Green Man can be evoked and honored in our own time. After a meditation in the woods, the figure was fashioned from branches. Then elastic bands were attached in order to decorate it with flowers and greenery as the center of a shrine.

These various versions of the folk plays have been collected from oral tradition in the same way that folk songs and folk tales have been. They are hard to date accurately, and no one has proved conclusively how old they are. At any rate, they are constantly updated with contemporary references—mostly political or personal—added by each local group. Invaluable as living vehicles for the preservation of pre-Christian traditions, they hold the final key to our quest for the Green Man.

The plays fall roughly into two categories: the hero combat and the sword dance. (These elements have tended to separate, so that now a sword dance is often performed independently from a drama.)

RIGHT AND BELOW: The Green Man returns to the streets at Perchtenlauf, Austria, dressed in ferns and fir cones.

THE HERO COMBAT

The Christianized hero play is often called the St. George play, since he is the main protagonist. But the name "George," like the names of the other characters, has changed through the centuries. The hero of the play has, in fact, had *many* names, including "Robin Hood," "Green Jack," and the "Wildman." The fact that in parts of Europe St. George is known as "Green George" suggests that at one time the hero may have been represented by a figure dressed in green, and that when the saint became identified with this character the color remained.

A reconstruction of the Northamptonshire

In the hero play George fights a battle with a villain who has had even more names than he. Among the most repeated are "The Turkish Knight," "The Turkish Champion," "Black Prince," "Bold Slasher," "Captain Slasher," "Cutting Star," "Swish Swish and Swagger," "Valiant Soldier," and so on.

One of the two combatants is killed (not always St. George), and a comedic doctor is called upon to bring him back to life. This is generally an excuse for much farcical behavior, with the "doctor" administering an enema to his "patient." In the original versions, this part would have been played by the village shaman, and the wounded man by a genuinely sick person.

> Various versions of the folk plays have been collected from oral tradition in the same way that folk songs and folk tales have been.

Mummers Play, originally collected by the poet John Clare and now known only in a fragmentary version, makes the identity of the two figures unequivocal.

> *In comes I, St. George is my name*
> *With my trusty sword, I am going to gain,*
> *If I could meet the Saracen knight here.*
> *I'd fight him and smite him and strike off his ear!*
> *Yes, I am St. George, and I'm the Green Man,*
> *And I will fight evil wherever I can!*

THE SWORD DANCE

The sword dance is a more complex affair in which the mummers themselves, or a second group of five or six men, perform an elaborate dance with long flexible blades. The dancers weave in and out in a slowly tightening circle until one of their number is caught at the center with his head poking up through an interlaced pattern of swords. To cries of "Chop! Chop! Chop!" or "A nut! A nut!" the swords are swiftly withdrawn and the victim falls down as though dead, at which point the dancers lift the interwoven swords and display them to the gathered watchers. St. George is the ritual victim in this dance in at least one version of the hero play traditionally performed at Midwinter, his return to life obviously symbolizing the anticipated rebirth of the natural world.

Once, the beheading was real, though it is also possible that even in ancient times the sacrifice was staged to allow the performers to demonstrate the "death" and "resurrection" of the victim, who represented the yearly cycle of the grain.

The phrase "A nut!" is actually a corruption of "knot!" We can see why this is so when we look closely at the pattern made by the interlocking swords. These form a five- or six-pointed star, which is similar to the symbol known as "Solomon's seal" or the "endless knot." This seal or knot was considered to be an image of divine wisdom and, significantly, was painted on Sir Gawain's shield in the poem of *Gawain and the Green Knight*. Its anonymous author lived in a part of England where the mummers plays would have been a common sight. They probably influenced his telling of a story that shares so vividly the underlying theme of the plays—the death and resurrection of the Green Man in his guise as the Year King.

JOHNNY APPLESEED

The Green Man has made a number of reappearances in the modern era. As we have seen, many of the European traditions discussed in this book are still celebrated in some regions of Britain. They are also practiced with revivalist vigor in some parts of the United States and Canada.

One of the most curious examples of a human being embodying the Green Man as the defining feature of his life is the eccentric American pioneer and nurseryman John Chapman (1774-1845), who came to be widely known as "Johnny Appleseed." He has reached almost mythical status in folk tradition as an American "St. Francis" and as a voice of the wilderness.

From the early 1790s on, Chapman worked his way west from his native Massachusetts to the Pennsylvania-Indiana-Ohio frontier, planting apple nurseries and spreading the words of the Gospel as interpreted by the Swedish mystic Emmanuel Swedenborg. Befriending and winning the respect of settlers and Native Americans alike, he served as kind of traveling shaman or medicine man. His apple seeds, exchanged for food, cast-off clothing, and other articles, supplied his simple needs, while whatever profits he made went into his purchase and dissemination of copies of the works of Swedenborg, a man whose own remarkable vision spoke of a living energy flowing through the universe.

Generally pictured as a bearded, barefoot, kindly hermit, with a tin mushpot and a linen coffee sack at his back, Chapman left a trail of anecdotes and legends, folk memories and public memorials, orchards and monuments, throughout the Middle West and

Johnny exchanged his apple seeds for food, cast-off clothing, and other articles to supply his simple needs.

ABOVE: This stained-glass window from Sherborne Abbey, Dorset, portrays a green shepherd in a Nativity scene.
RIGHT: Artist Mary Fedden shows the Green Man in his timeless role as the protector and husbandman of nature.

Fedden 1998

from coast to coast. He has been celebrated in drama, poetry, fiction, and biography as a virtual saint and memorialized by Church and horticultural societies alike as an inspired missionary. As a guiding light in the savage frontier world, he occupies a unique place in the pantheon of American folk heroes. This extraordinary visionary carried with him the seeds of more than his apples. He represented the first stirrings of a new awakening to a more simple way of life. Like John Muir, who pioneered the national parks movement in North America, Chapman was a pioneer who honored the Green Man as an expression of beliefs he felt from the center of his soul.

A NEW GREEN WORLD

As mentioned earlier, the Green Man has become an unofficial icon of the environmental movement—which tacitly acknowledges the importance of this ancient archetype to its work.

The contemporary poet Bill Lewis accurately sums up something of the attitude of environmentally conscious people today:

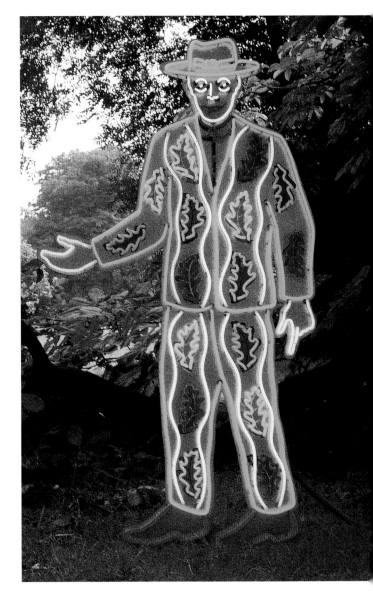

Powerplant and plantpower,
Green heart of the greenwood.
Larders and laboratories,
living libraries of herb lore.
Changes climatic and chemical
of solar flares and rainfall
recorded in treetrunks,
those mandalas of history. . . .
An invasion of sycamore,
A stand-fast of oak and a
blaze of beech in
fiery photo-synthesis.
If we uproot you then
we ourselves are uprooted;
and the greenman wears
a crown of thorns.
Arms outstretched
on a Calvary of antlers.
(*Greenheart*, 1996)

The contemporary men's movement, which seeks to redress the emphasis placed on feminine archetypes in recent years, has placed the Green Man at the heart of its reemerging symbolic landscape as a representative of masculine virility and potency. The leaders of this movement have formed societies which are a close equivalent of the ancient male groups from which the mummers emerged. They often lead retreats into the wilderness to help men reconnect with the masculine energy of the natural world.

Green Man iconography in her last lecture on the subject, saying that these plants:

> *. . . seem to have been observed directly from nature. This was an extraordinary innovation, since a love of nature was at variance with the teaching of the Church which tended to regard all plants and brute nature as belonging to the Devil. . . . Native plants . . . are suddenly recognised with pleasure, and the carvings often reflect objective curiosity and sheer sensuous pleasure.*
>
> (Basford, *Quest for the Green Man,* 1997)

The Church believed that nature was inherently evil. But among the common people, the spirit of nature continued to be celebrated as at least potentially divine. The greenery used in the carving of the foliate heads represented a conscious choice on the part of the artisans—a choice of sacred plants. It is as though the carvers were saying: "This is a sacred figure. Let us use sacred plants to represent him." In other parts of Europe the same choice was made. In Germany, for example, foliate heads are said to represent the *Zapfenmanndl*, a man dressed in fir cones, while in the form of the *Vershmanndl* he is covered in lichens, which are among the oldest genera of plant life.

The Green Man is a mediator between the worlds of humanity, vegetation, and animality. Informing all three aspects of creation, he is able to communicate the deeper meaning of the natural world to us, acting as a bridge between ourselves and that other world from which we have separated ourselves. We may have forgotten our place in the scheme of things, but we can be reeducated by this timeless archetype. If we really want to learn about the green world, we can turn to the Green Man as a teacher whose credentials are unique in the spirituality of our species.

NATURE'S VOICE

The leaves that sprout from and decorate the foliate heads of the Green Man are what constitutes them. These heads can be seen as an attempt by the artists who carved them to express the spirit of nature as a bearded, patriarchal figure—as a "god" of the woodlands and hedgerows. Nor is it accidental that these heads are often composed of the most common plants—vine, hops, hawthorn, bryony, buttercup, maple, and mugwort. The author Kathleen Basford mentioned the importance of these plants to the

TESTS OF THE GREEN MAN

The Green Man speaks green words, and his power is green power. He utters the syllables of the seasons, and his story is the cycle of the seasonal round. But he is not merely a *symbol* of nature's virility; rather he is a *direct manifestation* of it. He is also its guardian and champion. As we saw in the story of the Green Knight, one of the most important aspects of our relationship to the Green Man are the challenges and tests he offers us. From these we can learn much, not only about the natural world and its needs but also about ourselves.

The Green Man gives us an opportunity to reawaken to the spirit and intelligence of nature— the nature both within us and around us. But this can happen only if we allow it to, only if we overcome the negative aspects of ourselves that have separated us from the natural world—greed, materialism, too great a veneration of science, and a belief that the earth is ours to abuse however and whenever we wish. It takes courage to face our depredations and sacriledges. It is no longer enough simply to say: I deplore the ruination. Rather, we must each take responsibility in recovering a *real sense* of the *sacredness* of the earth.

GREEN MAN RISING

The age-old Green Man is coming back in our own time for a reason—urgently reminding us of our irrevocable relationship with our environment. Whether we acknowledge it or not, we are forever profoundly connected to the forces he represents— and, as I've said before, we neglect them at our peril. Nature has its own ways of hitting back—through "natural disasters" such as famine, plague, and drought. Paradoxically, we could simultaneously view these events as man-made disasters since more often than not our own neglect or mistreatment of the ecosystem invokes them.

We can reconnect with nature in a number of ways: through personal acts of conservation and care for our surroundings; by taking peaceful action to remind others of the damage they are doing and what they—indeed, what *all* of us—can do together to redress the balance. Perhaps more fundamentally, in our own private way we can honor the Green Man's presence, in whatever form seems most appropriate. This may mean nothing more than creating a small shrine as suggested in chapter 1. As the ecologist and writer Terry Tempest Williams has wisely said: "Ecology, like poetry, should be practiced by everyone."

If enough of us do so, we will see a change. It may be only slight, especially in the beginning, and we may yet see an even greater tide of destruction than we do now. But if we persevere, the day will surely come when we can offer our children a deeper connection to reality than they will ever find in the barren and shuttered world in which we presently live. Acknowledging the Green Man is only the first step, but it is an immensely important one. If you look back over the pages of this book, you will, I hope, see why. In the vibrant images and powerful stories contained here—and through the meditations presented as springboards for your own imaginal ventures—you will begin to resonate once more with the most ancient, and innate, patterns of being.

*ABOVE: The Jolly Green Giant from this advertising poster became an image of taste and quality during the early twentieth century.
RIGHT: Ever returning in different guises, the Green Man can be found watching over gardens, as in this relief by David Holmes.*

At the beginning of this book I suggested that to go out into the landscape was to become conscious of the Green Man's presence and that we might, if we listened, hear the song of the earth on every side. This is certainly true, but how much better it can be, how much more deeply we can relate to our environment, is something we discover best when we attune ourselves to the earth at a soul level. This is what St. Hildegard meant by viriditas, the greenness of the soul. If we ourselves listen to the voice of the Green Man, in whatever form he most appeals to us, we can begin to respond ever more deeply.

PRACTICE

A RITUAL JOURNEY

As we have seen, the characters representing the Green Man often have feminine counterparts or consorts. Together, four such partnerships of the Green Man/Green Woman form a seasonal and directional glyph that can help orient us to the values they embody. Each figure stands for an aspect of a particular season and direction, and each one presents a test or trial. Moving around the circle of the year as shown on page 137, they are as follows:

The Green Man of the **North** and of **Winter** is the **Green Knight**, who charges into King Arthur's court in the medieval poem, *Sir Gawain and the*

> Spending a little time each day considering your life in the light of the Green Man's presence may lead to transformative insights.

Green Knight. The test he poses is the challenge of death, metaphorically—that is, of dying to an old way of being in order to be reborn into a new way. For each of us, the challenge takes different forms. But in every case, we are asked to lose our lives in the sense that we give up our overconcern for ourselves as individuals and suffer the sometimes painful awakening to the energies of the greater world. To accept the challenge of the Green Knight entails reestablishing our connectedness with all life—animal and vegetable as well as human. This is the first stage in restoring the Green Man's voice and learning what he has to teach.

The Green Woman in consort with the Green Knight is **Lady Bercilak**, the wife of Gawain's host. Few who have read her story will forget her beauty and grace, as well as her bold sensuality. Her test is

that of the senses and of honesty, forcing us to come to terms with our approach to the physicality of our lives. Gawain deals well with her, in spite of his fear about his upcoming trial, and wins her respect.

The Green Man of the **East** and of **Spring** is **Robin Hood**. On the one hand he is a medieval outlaw, hiding in Sherwood forest with his band

of merry men, but on the other, he is a far more ancient figure whose role is to guard and care for the groves of the greenwood and its denizens, both human and animal.

There is a clear cycle to Robin's life: he enters the wood at springtime, where he is crowned the

May Day King. As such he rules for a year, accepting challenges from powerful otherworldly figures, each of whom he defeats and each of whom subsequently becomes part of his merry band. He also has to face the nameless Champion of Winter, with whom he must battle to win the hand of the Spring Maiden, here known as Maid Marian. Robin himself is a Green Gome, living deep in the wildwood and wearing a horned headdress, from which he becomes known as Robin-i-the-Hood, a ritual title dating from before the Middle Ages.

even split his first arrow with a second—a rare feat indeed. Skills of this kind are almost supernatural; and anyone who has ever shot an arrow with a longbow knows that pulling the clothyard shaft back to the cheek, and sighting along it provides a powerful lesson in focusing, an exercise in the clearsighted aiming of the spirit.

BELOW: The blossom of the crab apple in late spring. The apple is an important symbol in many spiritual traditions: it is Aphrodite's symbol; it was sacred to the Celts and revered by the Druids.

Robin's challenge is less obvious than that of the Green Knight. But if we consider the skill for which he is traditionally celebrated, we will see how it fits into the pattern of test and trial. Robin is, above all, a master at the use of the longbow. He can not only hit the center of the target every time, he can

So Robin's test is that of learning to aim one's spiritual intent with both discipline and insight. Without this inner direction we can never proceed toward a proper understanding of our place in the greater scheme of things. This is the second stage of restoring the Green Man's voice and learning what it is he has to teach us. Robin Hood's partner is, of course, **Maid Marian**, the May Queen, the consort of the King of the Wood. She exudes an unmistakable gentleness, gaiety, and sense of fun. She dances her way through life. Her test is the test of true love, of utter selflessness. She is best honored in her bower, a shelter woven of green branches and decorated with May blossom. As Queen of the May she brings a powerful feminine energy, matching the masculine energy of her Lord.

The Green Man of the **South** and of **Summer** is **Gromer Somer Jour**, whose name fittingly means "man of the summer's day." We recall that he is Arthur's formidable opponent who asks the riddle in the medieval poem, *The Wedding of Sir Gawain and the Dame Ragnall*. In many ways, he is the mirror reflection of the winter aspect of the Green Man—the Green Knight against whom Gawain must struggle. Both Gromer and the Green Knight are powerful otherworldly challengers, and both pose tests that require a change in conciousness in order to pass them.

Gromer's test is one of truth. To face him is to see oneself revealed in the clear light of the sun and so to see all the faults and cracks in the facade of one's human nature. We often present ourselves to the world one way, but our inner reality may be very different. The test in this quarter is to see ourselves as we really are, and to make whatever

changes may be necessary in light of this truthful approach. Gromer's test is the third stage in restoring a voice to the Green Man and of learning what he has to teach.

Gromer's partner is **Lady Ragnall**. Given the appearance of a hideous woman by Morgana, Ragnall must find a man willing to give her the freedom to choose. Her test is the test of free will. It is not until Gawain gives her the right to be herself that she is freed from the oppression of Morgane's spell. We might think of her as a representative of the earth, an earth that will only be set free when we give it the right to follow its own course of development rather than our dictates.

Lastly, the Green Man of the **West** and of **Autumn** is the **Green Jack**, the wild and ungovernable figure who can be seen in towns and villages throughout Britain at key times of the year. As we have seen, he is also known as Jack-in-the-Green, the Burryman, John Barleycorn, and Robin Goodfellow. He is primarily a trickster who plays pranks on people, dances wildly in the streets, is "cut down" and "rises" again, and is sacrificed to assure an abundant harvest. He stands as the mirror image of Robin Hood in the East.

The Jack's test is a simple one: that of dying in order to awaken to new life and trusting in your rebirth. However, this test is not the same as the Green Knight's challenge, for to take the role of the Jack is to suffer psychic or spiritual death, to remain

Let the unfolding of the mystery bring you replenishment and understanding of the way of the Green Man.

a while in the Underworld and then to return, bringing knowledge and healing to the people and the land. Submission to this metamorphosis requires trusting that if you embrace this death, you will return. Without passing this test of trust, we cannot live even a moment of our lives with any significant degree of peace. This is the fourth and final stage in restoring the Green Man's voice and of learning what it is he has to teach us.

In Autumn, Green Jack's partner is the **Harvest Queen**, who gathers the rich crop of grain, berries, and fruits in her cornucopia. In the archetype of the Harvest Queen we may discern the ancient Goddess of the Grain; but these days she is most often seen in the corn dollies that are braided from the last sheaf harvested from the fields and made into an effigy of the Harvest Queen, trimmed with ribbons. Her test is the struggle for survival in the face of want. While Green Jack as John Barleycorn is cut down and made into beer and whiskey, the Harvest Queen is made into the bread that will feed us through the winter.

Together, they bring the cycle back full circle to the North. We can represent all these different aspects of the Green Man and his consort, the Green Woman, in a diagram, similar to that with which we began this book (see page 10).

Having set up the four quarters in this way with their various powers and qualities, we can prepare to make a journey to one or the other of these directions, there to communicate with one of the several beings about whom we have read.

You can do this by turning to the direction of your choice and closing your eyes. Concentrate deeply on the figure to whom you feel most drawn. Perhaps one of them will seek you out! Imagine yourself in the forest, or in the green fields of standing corn, or seated by a river, or walking on the hills with the wind blowing through your hair. Imagine yourself walking or sitting in one of those places, and take time to be with the being you have chosen—or who has chosen you. The rest is between you and this representative of the Green Man. Each has something different to teach you about healing both yourself and the earth. Each one, as we have seen, offers a specific test. You may, if you wish, commit yourself to this test, at first in the inner realm of your imagination, later in the outer world. Or you may simply ask the figure what it has to teach, and how you can help to restore the Green Man's voice.

In time, you might visit all these figures, learning from each of them. Take your time, and let the gradual unfolding of the mystery bring you replenishment and insight into the way of the Green Man.

NORTH
WINTER
THE GREEN KNIGHT
LADY BERCILAK

WEST
AUTUMN
GREEN JACK
THE HARVEST QUEEN

EAST
SPRING
ROBIN HOOD
MAID MARIAN

SOUTH
SUMMER
GROMER SOMER JOUR
LADY RAGNALL

ABOVE LEFT: A modern vision of the Green Man by artist Courtney Davis draws upon Celtic imagery for inspiration.

ABOVE: This diagram shows how the partnership of the Green Man and the Green Woman form a seasonal and directional gylph.

Sources and Resources

Despite the large number of writings on the Green Man and associated subjects there is still no comprehensive listing of carvings and suchlike. Several of the books listed in the bibliography contain partial listings, including Kathleen Basford's seminal book, and Ronald Millar's *Green Man: Companion and Gazeteer*. The last named has also formed The Company of the Green Man, which actively seeks out and reports on Green Man sightings and produces a quarterly newsletter. For more information on this, or to join, write to:
Ronald Millar, The Tower, Wappingthorne Farm, Horsham Road, Steyning, West Sussex, BN44 3AA, UK

Further excellent lists, including sites outside the area of this work, may be found in Peter Hill's excellent *In Search of the Green Man in Northamptonshire* (Orman Publishing, 1999) and in Clive Hicks' *Green Man: A Gazeteer* (Compass Books, 2000).

In addition to these resources, Ruth Wylie of Hampshire, England, is also compiling an international list. To find out more about this write to her at:
Ruth Wylie, Moray, 100 Furze Hill Road, Headley Down, Bordon, Hampshire. GU35 8HD, UK

Some of her excellent photographs, along with a brief article on the Green Man, can be viewed on the website maintained by Albion Press (also an excellent source for Green Man and related materials) at:
indigogroup.co.uk/edge/greenman.htm

Some more striking Green Man and Green Woman images can be found on the site maintained by Terri Windling at:
endicottStudio.com/galgreen.html

Though by no means comprehensive, these resources should be sufficient to keep the most driven Green Man enthusiasts busy for several years. A full gazeteer is still badly needed, and though the present author is unable to undertake this work he is always interested in hearing from those who have found "new" Green Man sightings and will endeavor to pass on all such information to the appropriate people. You can write to him at:
BCM Hallowquest, London WC1X 3XX.

EVENTS

For readers in the USA there is still comparatively little by way of Green Man activities. However, one excellent source of Green Man and related subjects are the wonderful Revels groups which have sprung up across much of North America in recent years. A list of the main groups can be found in my book *The Winter Solstice*, or direct from their website at:
www.revels.org
Or write to:
Revels Inc., One Kendall Square, Bldg 600, Cambridge, MA 02139, USA

Though devoted primarily to the celebration of Solstice events, some groups may be more oriented toward Green Man activities than others. It is well worth seeking out such groups in your area and getting in touch with them.

For those living in or visiting the UK, there are a number of events which take place regularly throughout the year. These include a Green Man festival at Clun in Shropshire; a Sweeps Festival at Rochester in Kent; and a Jack-in-the-Green Festival at Hastings in Sussex. In addition, the Abbots Bromley Horn Dance is performed each September at the village of Abbots Bromley in Staffordshire. Numerous Morris dances and Mumming Plays are held throughout the country on May Day and at Christmas. One of the best (and oldest) of these plays is performed by the Headington Morris in Oxford. (Details are available from the local Tourist Office.)

In Scotland, at South Queensferry you can still see the Burryman led through the streets in August. In Whittlesea, near Peterborough in Yorkshire, the Straw Bear passes through the streets in January. There are in addition a large number of local folk customs taking place throughout the year in Britain, many of which are listed in such excellent books as *The Perpetual Almanack of Folk Lore* or *The Customs and Ceremonies of Britain*, both by Charles Kightly (for details see Further Reading).

GREEN MAN IMAGES

In addition, for those who would like to possess a Green Man of their own, there are a number of excellent craftspeople who are producing carvings or paintings of Green Men. Most of these will accept commissions or have existing work for sale. Those who are interested might like to contact the following:
Allen Calvin, 29 Gilmour Place, Hamilton, Ontario, L8M 2Y3, Canada
Fleur Fitzgerald, 3 Christmas Pie Ave, Normandy, Surrey, GU3 2EQ, UK
David Holmes, Plymouth, Maine

The Goddess and the Green Man in Glastonbury, Somerset, sells and exports Green Men and Goddess carvings throughout the world. Write to them for an illustrated catalog at:
The Goddess and the Green Man, 2 High Street, Glastonbury, Somerset BA6 9DU, UK

In the USA there is:
The Hobbit Doorway, 362 Main Street, Athol, MA 01331, USA

On the Web take a look at The Mythic Images Collection at:
www.mythicimages.com

COURSES

John and Caitlín Matthews give regular courses in Europe and the USA on Shamanic, Arthurian, and Celtic traditions. They also produce a quarterly newsletter. For a sample issue, write, enclosing 8 first-class stamps (UK), or a U.S. $5 bill to:
BCM Hallowquest, London, WC1X 3XX.
The newsletter is also available in electronic format at *Hallowquest.org.uk*

Further Reading

Alexander, M. *British Folklore, Myths and Legends*. Weidenfeld & Nicholson, 1982.

Alford, V. *Sword Dance and Drama*. London, 1962.

Alford, V. *The Hobby Horse & Other Animal Masks*. London, 1978.

Allen, Romilly. *Norman Sculpture and the Medieval Bestiaries*. 1887 (reprinted Llanerch: Llanerch Publishers, c.1990).

Amerie, Robert. *Chesters Triumph in Honour of Her Prince*. London, 1610.

Andersen, Jorgen. *The Witch on the Wall: Medieval Erotic Sculpture in the British Isles*. London: Allen and Unwin, 1977.

Anderson, M.D. *History and Imagery in British Churches*. John Murray, 1971.

Anderson, W. *Green Man: The Archetype of our Oneness with the Earth*. Harper Collins, 1990.

Bailey, H. *Archaic England*. Chapman and Hall, 1919.

Bancroft, Anne. *Origins of the Sacred*. London: Arkana, 1987.

Banks, M.M. *British Calendar Customs*. London: Keegan Paul, Trench, Tubner, 1937.

Bartra, Roger. *Wild Men in the Looking Glass: The Mythic Origins of European Otherness*. Ann Arbor: The University of Michigan Press, 1994.

Basford, K. "A New View of 'Green Man' Sculptures." *Folklore* 102 (1991): 237–9.

Basford, K. *The Green Man*. Cambridge: Boydell & Brewer,1978.

Basford, K. "The Quest for the Green Man." In *Symbols of Power*. Ed. by H.R.E. Davidson. Brewer/Roman & Littlefield, 1977.

Bate, John. *The Mysteries of Nature and Art*. London, 1637.

Bernheimer, R. *Wild Men in the Middle Ages*. Cambridge, Mass.,1952.

Betty, J.H. and C.W.G. Taylor. *Sacred and Satiric: Medieval Stone Carving in the West Country*. Redcliffe, 1982.

Bishop, Peter. *The Greening of Psychology*. Dallas, Texas: Spring Publications, 1990.

Blackwood, John. *Oxford's Gargoyles and Grotesques*. Charon Press, 1986.

Blackwood, John. *Windsor Castle's Gargoyles and Grotesques*. Charon Press, 1988.

Bleakley, Alan. *Fruits of the Moon Tree*. London: Gateway Books, 1984.

Bord, J. & C. *Earth Rites: Fertility Practices in Pre-Industrial Britain*. Granada,1982.

Bord, J. & C. *Mysterious Britain*. Granada,1974.

Brand, J. *Observations on the Popular Antiquities of Great Britain* (3 vols). George Bell & Sons,1908.

Briggs, K. *A Dictionary of Fairies*. Alan Lane, 1976.

Brighton, Christopher. *Lincoln Cathedral Cloister Bosses*. Honywood Press, 1985.

Brodie, A. *The English Mummers and their Plays*. Routledge & Kegan Paul, 1970.

Buchan, P. *Ancient Scottish Tales*. Peterhead, Transactions of the Buchan Field Club, 1908.

Burbank, Lester Bridaham. *Gargoyles, Chimeres and the Grotesque in French Gothic Sculpture*. New York: Da Capa Press, 1969.

Burland, C. *Echoes of Magic*. Rowman & Littlefield,1972.

Carter, R.O.M. and H.M. "The foliate head in England." *Folklore* Vol. 78, pp. 269–74.

Cave, C.J.P. *Roof Bosses in Medieval Churches*. Cambridge University Press, 1948.

Cave, C.J.P. *Lincoln Roof Bosses*. 2nd ed. Friends of Lincoln Cathedral, 1951.

Cawte, E.C. *Ritual Animal Disguise*. Brewer/Roman and Littlefield, 1978.

Cervantes, Miguel de. *Don Quixote de la Mancha*. Translated by J.M. Cohen. Middlesex: Penguin Books, 1950.

Chambers, E. *English Literature at the Close of the Middle Ages*. Oxford University Press, 1947.

Chambers, E. *The English Folk Play*. Oxford University Press, 1933.

Chambers, E.K. *The Medieval Stage*. New York, Dover Publications, 1996.

Child, F.J. *English and Scottish Popular Ballads*. New York: Houghton Mifflin, 1882–1898.

Chretien de Troyes. *Arthurian Romances*. Trans. by W.W. Comfort. London: Dent, 1963.

Clawson, W.H. *The Gest of Robin Hood*. Toronto: University of Toronto Library, 1909.

Cooper, H. *Pastoral : Medieval into Renaissance*. D.S. Brewer/Rowman & Littlefield,1977.

Cooper, J.C. *The Aquarian Dictionary of Festivals*. Aquarian Press, 1990.

Cooper, Quentin. & P. Sullivan. *Maypoles, Martyrs & Mayhem*. London: Bloomsbury, 1994.

Cross, T.P. & C.H. Slover. *Ancient Irish Tales*. Dublin: C.W. Dunn,1969.

Danaher, Kevin. *The Year in Ireland*. Dublin, Mercier Press, 1972.

Dobson, R.B. & J. Taylor. *Rymes of Robyn Hood: An Introduction to the English Outlaw*. Alan Sutton,1989.

Douglas, Norman. *London Street Games*. London, 1916.

Douce, F. *Illustrations of Shakespeare*. London, 1807.

Duffy, M. *The Erotic World of the Faery*. Hodder & Stoughton, 1972.

Ferguson, John. *The Religions of the Roman Empire*. London: Thames & Hudson,1970.

Flecknoe, Richard. *Rich. Flecknoe's Aenigmatical Characters*. London, 1665.

Fowler, D.C. *A Literary History of the Popular Ballad*. Durham: North Carolina, 1968.

Fraser, J.G. *The Golden Bough* (abridged edition). Macmillan, 1974.

Gardham, Jane. *The Green Man*. Illus. by Mary Fedden. Gloucestershire: The Windrush Press, 1998.

Goulstone, J. *The Summer Solstice Games*. Privately Printed, 1985.

Green, Joyce Conyngham. *Salmagundi: Being a Calendar of Sundry Matters*. London: J.M. Dent, 1947.

Green, Marian. *A Calendar of Festivals*. Shaftsbury: Element Books, 1991.

Green, M. *A Harvest of Festivals*. Longmans, 1980.

Groesinger, Christa. *The World Upside Down: English Misericords*. Harvey Miller, 1997.

Groom, F.H. *Gypsey Folk-Tales*. London, 1899.

Grundy, Thirlie. *Cry Pure, Cry Pagan in Carlisle Cathedral*. Thumbprint, 1995.

Grundy, Thirlie. *The Misericord Carvings in Chester Cathedral*. Thumbprint, 1995.

Grundy, Thirlie. *The Misericord Carvings in the Cathedral Church of St Nicholas, Newcastle upon Tyne*. Thumbprint, 1995.

Grundy, Thirlie. *The Misericord Carvings in the Cathedral Church of Exeter*. Thumbprint, 1995.

Grundy, Thirlie. *The Misericord Carver of Hexham Abbey*. Thumbprint, 1997.

Guest, Lady C. *The Mabinogion*. J.M. Dent, 1937.

Gurevich, Aron. *Medieval Popular Culture: Problems of Belief and Perception*. Trans. J.M. Bak. Cambridge UP, 1988.

Hampson, R.T. *Kalendars of the Middle Ages*. London: Henry Kent Causton. n.d.

Harding, Mike. *A Little Book of the Green Man*. London, Aurum Press, 1998.

Harrison, Alan. "The Green Men of Charente [France]." *RILKO Journal* No. 48 (1996): 15–17.

Harrison, J. *Ancient Art and Ritual*. Thornton Butterworth, 1918.

Harrison, Robert Pogue. *Forests: The Shadow of Civilization*. Chicago and London: University of Chicago Press, 1992.

Harrowven, J. *Origins of Rhymes, Songs and Sayings*. Kaye & Ward, 1977.

Henderson, H. "The Green Man of Knowledge." *Scottish Studies 2*. (1958): 47–85.

Head, Barry. "The Incredible Green Man." *Yorkshire Life* 34, No. 9 (September 1980): 54–5.

Hill, Peter. *In Search of the Green Man in Northamptonshire*. Orman, 1996.

Hilton, R.H. "The Origins of Robin Hood." *Past & Present* 14 (1958): 30–44.

Hole, C. *A Dictionary of British Folk Customs*. Hutchinson, 1976.

Hole, C. *English Folk Heroes*. Batsford, 1948.

Hull, E. *Folklore of the British Isles*. Methuen, 1928.

Husband, T. *The Wild Man: Medieval Myth & Symbolism*. New York: Metropolitan Museum of Art, 1980.

Hutton, Ronald. *The Rise & Fall of Merry England*. Oxford: Oxford University Press, 1995.

Hutton, Ronald. *The Stations of the Sun: A History of the Ritual Year in Britain*. Oxford: Oxford University Press, 1996.

Hyde, Walter. *Paganism to Christianity in the Roman Empire*. Philadelphia: University of Pennsylvania Press, 1946.

James, E.O. *Seasonal Feasts & Festivals*. Thames & Hudson, 1961.

Johnson, Ronald. *The Book of the Green Man*. London, Longmans, 1967.

Judge, R. *The Jack in the Green*. Boydell & Brewer/Roman & Littlefield, 1979.

Judge, Roy. "The Green Man Revisited." *Colour and Appearance in Folklore*. Ed. J. Hutchings and J. Wood. London: The Folklore Society, 1991, pp 51–5.

Jung, C. G. *Symbols of Transformation*. Trans. by R.F.C. Hull. London: Routledge & Kegan Paul, 1967.

Keen, M. *The Outlaws of Medieval Legend*. London: Routledge & Kegan Paul, 1977.

Keightley, T. *The Fairy Mythology*. Wildwood House, 1981.

Kennedy, P. *England's Dances*. G. Bell, 1950.

Kennedy, Peter (ed.) *Folk-Songs of Britain & Ireland*. London: Cassell, 1975.

Kightly, C. *The Customs & Ceremonies of Britain*. Thames & Hudson, 1986.

Kightly, C. *The Perpetual Almanack of Folk-Lore*. Thames & Hudson, 1987.

King, John. *The Celtic Druid's Year*. London: Blandford Press, 1996.

Kinsley, J. (ed.) *The Oxford Book of Ballads*. Oxford University Press, 1969.

Kirtlan, E.J.B. *Sir Gawain & the Green Knight*. Kelly, 1912.

Larwood, Jacob and John Camden Hotten. *The History of Signboards, from Earliest Times to the Present Day*. London: J.C. Hotten, 1866.

Lehrs, Max. *Late Gothic Engravings of Germany and the Netherlands*. New York: Dover Publications, 1969.

Lewis, Bill. *Greenheart*. London: Lazerwolf, 1996.

Lilywhite, Bryant. *London Signs*. London: George Allen and Unwin, 1972.

Lloyd, A.L. *Folk Song in England*. Paladin, 1975.

Lonsdale, Steven. *Animals & the Origins of Dance*. Thames & Hudson, 1981.

Long, George. *The Folklore Calendar*. London: Philip Allen, 1930.

Lurker, Manfred. *The Gods and Symbols of Ancient Egypt*. London: Thames & Hudson, 1980.

Malory, T. *Le Morte d'Arthur*. Ed. John Matthews. London: Orion, 2000.

Mann, Nicholas R. *His Story*. St. Paul, MN: Llewellyn Publications, 1995.

Marvin W. *The Ancient Mysteries : A Sourcebook*. San Francisco: Harper & Row, 1987.

Matthews, C. *Arthur and the Sovereignty of Britain*. Arkana, 1989.

Matthews, Caitlín. *The Celtic Book of Days*. London: Godsfield Press, 1995.

Matthews, Caitlín. *Celtic Devotional*. London: Godsfield Press, 1996.

Matthews, Caitlín. *Elements of the Celtic Tradition*. Shaftsbury: Element Books, 1996.

Matthews, C. *Mabon and the Mysteries of Britain*. Arkana, 1987.

Matthews, J. *A Bardic Source-Book*. London: Cassell, 1998.

Matthews, J. *A Celtic Reader*. London: Harper Collins, 1995.

Matthews, J. *The Celtic Shaman*. Element Books, 1991.

Matthews, J. *A Druid Source-Book*. London: Cassell, 1997.

Matthews, J. *Gawain: Knight of the Goddess*. Aquarian Press, 1990.

Matthews, J. *Robin Hood: Green Lord of the Wildwood*. Glastonbury: Gothic Image Publications, 1996.

Matthews, J. *Taliesin: Shamanism & the Bardic Mysteries in Britain and Ireland*. Harper Collins, 1990.

Matthews, J. with R.J. Stewart. *Legendary Britain*. Cassell, 1989.

Mayfield, Beatrice. *Apple Games & Customs*. London: Common Ground, 1994.

McNeill, F. M. *The Silver Bough* (4 Vols) Willam Maclellan, 1959.

McPherson, J.M. *Primitive Beliefs in the North-East of Scotland.* Meyer, Longmans, Green & Co, 1929.

Millar, Ronald. *The Green Man: Companion & Gazeteer.* Seaford: S.B. Publications, 1997.

Mottram, E. *The Book of Herne.* Arrowspire Press, 1981.

Murray, M. *The Divine King in England.* Faber & Faber, 1954.

Murray, M. *The God of the Witches.* Oxford University Press, 1952.

Nutt, A. *The Fairy Mythology of Shakespear.* David Nutt, 1900.

Pennick, Nigel. *Crossing the Borders.* Chieveley: Capall Bann Publishing, 1998.

Pennick, Nigel. *The Pagan Source Book.* London: Rider, 1992.

Petry, M.J. *Herne the Hunter.* Privately Printed, Reading, 1972.

Raglan, Lady J. "The 'Green Man' in Church Architecture." *Folklore* 50 (1939):45–57.

Raglan, Lord. *The Hero.* Watts & Co., 1949.

Rhys, E. *Fairy Gold: A Book of Old English Fairy Tales.* J.M.Dent, n.d.

Ritson, J. *Robin Hood: A Collection of all the Ancient Poems, Songs and Ballads Now Extant.* C. Stocking, 1823.

Rose, Martial, and Julia Hedgecoe. *Stories in Stone: the Medieval Roof Carvings of Norwich Cathedral* London: Herbert Press, c.1996.

Santillana, G. & H. Von Dechend. *Hamlet's Mill.* Macmillan, 1969.

Senior, Alan. "Masked Messengers." *Scottish Memories* (December 1996): 33–4.

Sheridan, Ronald and Anne Ross. *Grotesques and Gargoyles: Paganism in the Medieval Church.* London: David and Charles, 1975.

Simek, Rudolf. *Dictionary of Northern Mythology.* Cambridge: D.S. Brewer, 1993.

Simeone, W.E. "The May-Games and the Robin Hood Legend." *Journal of American Folk-Lore* 64 (1951): 265–74.

Sitwell, S. *Primitive Scenes & Festivals.* Faber, 1942.

Skelton, R & M. Blackwood. *Earth, Air, Fire, Water.* Arkana, 1991.

Spence, L. *British Fairy Origins.* Aquarian Press, 1981.

Spence, L. *The Fairy Tradition in Britain.* Rider, 1948.

Spence, L. *The Minor Traditions in British Mythology.* Rider, 1948.

Spence, L. *Myth and Ritual in Dance, Game and Rhyme.* Watts, 1947.

Spence, L. "The Supernatural Character of Robin Hood." *Hibbert Journal* XL (1947): 280–285.

Spittal, Michael. "The Green Man/Foliate Head." *Folklore Society News* 24 (1996): 8–9.

Strutt, Joseph. *The Sports and Pastimes of the People of England.* Ed. William Hone. London: Chatto and Windus, 1898.

Taubman, Matthew. *London's Yearly Jubilee.* London, 1686.

Thomas, K. *Religion & the Decline of Magic.* Penguin Books,1978.

Thomas, W.J. *Early English Prose Romances.* Routledge, 1898.

Trevelyan, M. *Folk-Lore and Folk-Stories of Wales.* Eliot Stock,1909.

Trubshaw, R.N. *Little-known Leicestershire and Rutland.* Heart of Albion Press, 1995.

Trubshaw, R.N. "The Green Men of Warmington" *Northamptonshire Local History News* Vol. III, No. 9 (Spring 1996): 1–3

Trubshaw, R.N. "The Facts and Fancies of the Foliate Face." *At the Edge* No. 4, (1996): 25–28.

Vansittart, P. *The Death of Robin Hood.* Peter Owen, 1981.

Vansittart, P. *Green Knights, Black Angels.* Macmillan, 1961.

Vansittart, P. *Worlds & Underworlds.* Peter Owen, 1974.

Von dem Turlin, H. *The Crown (Diu Crone).* Trans. by J.W. Thomas. University of Nebraska,1989.

Walker, J.W. *The True History of Robin Hood.* E.P. Publishing, 1973.

Weber-Kellerman, I. "Laubkonig und Schiossmeier: Geschichte und Deutung pfingstlichter Vegetationsgebritiche in Thuringen." *Deutsches Jahrbuch fur Volkskunde* 4 (1958): 366–85.

Webster, G. *The British Celts and their Gods Under Rome.* Batsford, 1986.

Weir, Anthony and James Jarman. *Images of Lust.* London: Batsford, 1986.

Welsford, E. *The Fool: His Social & Literary History.* Faber, 1935.

Wentz, W.Y. Evans. *Fairy Faith in Celtic Countries.* H. Frowde, 1911.

Wetherbee. W. *The Cosmographia of Bernardus Silvestris.* New York: Columbia Univ. Press, 1973.

Whetstone, George. *The Second Parte of the Famous History of Promos and Cassandra.* London: 1578.

White, Hayden. "The Forms of Wildness: Archaeology of an Idea." In *The Wild Man Within: An Image in Western Thought, from the Renaissance to Romanticism.* Ed. Edward Dudley and Maximillian E. Novak. Pittsburgh: University of Pittsburgh Press, 1972, pp. 3–38.

Whitlock, R. *In Search of Lost Gods.* Phaidon,1979.

Whitwell, Ben. "The Green Man: a Study." *Land, People and Landscape.* Ed. D. Tyszka, K. Miller and G. Bryant. Lincolnshire Books, 1991 (Lincolnshire examples)

Wiles, D. *The Early Plays of Robin Hood.* D.S. Brewer/Roman & Littlefield,1981.

Wilkins, Joan. "The Green Man." *Sussex History* No. 31, 1991.

Wilsher, Betty. "The Green Man in Scotland." *Circles* No 15 (1992): 12–17.

Williams, Terry Tempest. *Leap.* Pantheon Books, 2000.

Williamson, J. *The Oak King, the Holly King, and the Uniorn.* Harper & Row, 1986.

Wylie, Ruth "The Green Man: Variations on a Theme." *At the Edge* No.4 (1996): 20–24.

Wylie, Ruth. "The Green Man/Foliate Head." *Folklore Society News* 24 (1999): 11–12.

Index

Illustration Credits

Allen Calvin, p. 27 (photo John Sharp)
Ancient Art & Architecture Collection Ltd, pp. 24, 58
Andy Goldsworthy, p. 124
Anne Ross, pp. 23 (below), 110 (both)
Art Archive, pp. 29 (Egyptian Museum, Cairo), 116 (Dagli Orti)
Art Directors/Trip/J. Ringland, p. 73 (top)

Bildarchiv Foto Marburg, p. 92
Bill Lewis, p. 89 (below)
Brian Froud, p. 37
Bridgeman Art Library, pp. 49, 68 (below), 71, 72, 73 (below), 78/9 (Pieter Gysels, 1621–c.1691. Oil on copper), 89 (top), 98, 108, 119

Clive Hicks, pp. 14 (top), 18, 42, 45, 47, 66, 75 (below), 86, 131
CM Dixon, pp. 21 (right), 25, 46, 114
Collections, pp. 2 (Robin Weaver), 15 (Malcolm Crowthers), 70 (Brian Shuel), 74 (Brian Shuel), 80 (Brian Shuel), 94 (Ashley Cooper)
Common Ground, p. 130 (Sue Clifford)
Corinium Museum, Cirencester p. 34
Courtney Davis, p. 136

Donald Cooper/Photostage, p. 81

Felicity Bowers, pp. 39, 113
Fleur Fitzgerald, p. 6
Fortean Picture Library, pp. 16, 44, 56, 63 (Janet and Colin Bord), 77, 90 (Janet and Colin Bord), 96, 97, 100/101, 104, 106 (Janet and Colin Bord)
Freer Gallery of Art, Washington (Smithsonian Institute), p. 31 (1937.24)

Geraint ap Iowerth: by kind permission of the Rector and Churchwardens of St. Peter ad vincula, Pennal, Southern Snowdonia, p. 118
Giovanna Pierce, pp. 54-5, 64-5, 84-5, 102-3, 122-3

Harper & Row, p. 30
Homer Sykes/Network, pp. 14 (below), 77 (top)

Jane Brideson, p. 93
Jane Gifford, pp. back cover, 1, 19, 43, 67, 125, 134/135
Jeff Gresko, p. 126 (both)
John Matthews, pp. 69, 75 (top), 76
John Piper Estate, p. 17

Ian Adams, p. 133 and cover

Kathleen Basford, courtesy Common Ground p. 21 (left)
Kettle's Yard, University of Cambridge p. 52
Leiden University Library, p. 88 (Ltk 195, fol. 120v)

Mark Buckingham, p. 20
Mary Evans Picture Library, pp. 28, 36, 60 (top), 62, 68 (top), 99, 111, 115
Mary Fedden, pp. 83, 129
Michael Freeman, p. 33
Michael J. Stead, pp. 87, 95, 107, 121
Mick Sharp Photography, pp. 7, 26, 41, 51 (Jean Williamson), 105 (Jean Williamson)
Musée Suisse, Zürich, p. 35

Nigel Pennick, p. 127 (both)

Reproduced by permission of the Pillsbury Company, p. 132

Rheinisches Landesmuseum, Trier, p. 11
Roger Garland, p. 109
Ronald Grant Archive, pp. 50, 61
Rosslyn Chapel Trust, p. 38 (Antonia Reeve)

Courtesy SAC Ltd, p. 60
Schnütgen Museum, Köln, p. 112
Sonia Halliday Photographs, pp. 13, 53, 91 (both), 128
Staatliche Museum, Berlin, p. 32 (Ingrid Geske)
Städtische Galerie im Lensbachhaus, München, p. 120

Thames & Hudson, p. 23 (above)

Verulamium, St Albans, p. 117

Woodfall Wild Images, pp. 8-9, 22 (Mike Hartwell), 56. (David Woodfall), 59 (M. Hamblin)